First American Edition, 2019

Copyright 2019 The DIY Place Limited

All rights reserved.
Without limiting the rights under the copyright reserved above, no part of this publication may be reproduced, stored in or introduced into a retrieval system, or transmitted, in any form, or by any means (electronic, mechanical, photocopying, recording or otherwise), without the prior written permission of the copyright owner.

ISBN 978-1-943871-85-8
Published in the United States of America by
Painted Gate Publishing

Project Editors: Hokmah Communications

Template Designs: Chaela Wooding

Photography: Relate Studios

Note
The authors and publishers have made every effort to ensure that all instructions given in this book are safe and accurate, but they cannot accept liability for any resulting injury or loss or damage to either property or person, whether direct or consequential and however arising.

All images © The DIY Place Limited
For further information see: www.diyplace.org

Acknowledgements

As with any such endeavor, the support given by so many is greatly appreciated. Special thanks to my family and group of special friends who have helped to make this book a reality.

Art and Craft for Elementary School

Step by step instructions to make over fifty crafts.

Camille Wooding

We craft creative experiences

Foreword

Craft is a great way to complement teaching! This book is an easy text for teachers and homeschool parents as part of a holistic learning approach.

Free online videos complement this book, and help guide the craft making process allowing for ease of use in the classroom, or at home. We highly recommend teachers and children view the videos before starting to make the crafts.

We have included some very simple craft items and a few that are more complex. Each presents an opportunity for learning and exploring aspects of the school curriculum in Science, Social Studies, Mathematics, Language and of course, Art and Craft.

Teachers are encouraged to use craft to complement regular teaching.

We recommend adult supervision when making any of these projects.

The materials used in our crafts are affordable and readily available. We also use recyclable materials. In our videos, we often suggest alternative materials for some crafts. Templates are available at the back of the book.

Measurements are in imperial (inches/feet) with metric equivalents (centimetres/metres) in brackets, in some instances the equivalent metric is rounded for ease of use.

Our **Handy Dandy Craft Box** pairs perfectly with the book, as it contains a lot of the materials required to make the crafts. For ease of reference, these materials are identified separately in this book.

Check out our You Tube Channel to view videos on how to make all these projects.

So how do you use this book? Your child or students may have already figured it out. View the video, gather the materials and get started having fun!

…Be a maker

Table of Contents

Foreword	i
Introduction	1
Materials and Resources	3
The Handy Dandy Craft Box	3
Other Materials	4
Recyclables	4
Other Resources	5
Measurements	5
How to Trace a Template	6
Using Tracing Paper	6
Using Carbon or Graphite Paper	7
Playing with Paper	8
1. Nameplate	9
2. Idea Book	10
3. Caterpillar	11
4. Pinwheel	12
5. Folded Butterfly	14
6. Basket	15
7. Banner 1	16
8. Banner 2	18
9. Fan	20
10. Simple Kite	21
11. Heart Card	22
12. Candle Card	23
13. Carnation Flower	24
14. Jellyfish Sun Catcher	26
Playing with Paint	28
15. Patterns	29
16. Foam Stamping	30
17. Blot Painting	31
18. Painting with Lines	32
Playing with Paper Rolls	33
19. How to cover a paper roll	33
20. Butterfly Puppet	34
21. Bee Puppet	36
22. Robot Puppet	38
23. Ninja Puppets	39

24.	Microphone	40
25.	Lantern	41
26.	Paper Village	42
27.	Rainmaker	44

Playing with Sticks — 45

28.	Pencil Bookmark	45
29.	Foam Sticker Bookmark	46
30.	Critter Bookmark	47
31.	Airplane	48
32.	Pencil Topper	49
33.	Picture Frame	50
34.	Tree	51
35.	House Magnet	52
36.	Pencil Holder	53

Playing with Rocks — 54

37.	Painted Rocks	54
38.	Dominoes	55
39.	Tic Tac Toe Game (1)	56
40.	Rock Frame	57

Playing with Cardboard — 58

41.	Magazine / Book Holder	58
42.	Card/ Paper Holder	60
43.	Star Door Hanger	61
44.	Butterfly Mobile	62

Playing with Yarn — 64

45.	Tassels	64
46.	Pom Poms	66
47.	Ninja Star	67
48.	Friendship Bracelet	68
49.	Turtle	70

Playing with Fabric — 71

50.	Decorate your art bag	71
51.	Tic Tac Toe Game 2	72
52.	Patterned Tea Towel	73

Templates — 74

Introduction

Art and Craft for Elementary School contains 52, easy-to-make arts and crafts projects which can be made in the classroom.
Turtles and pinwheels and airplanes! All can be used as part of a holistic education model or done just for fun!

This book is excellent for school use, homeschool and makes a wonderful gift.

We guide readers through each project, giving step-by-step photos and instructions that kids will be able to follow.

Our free online videos give some added support for visual and auditory learners. Our Handy Dandy Craft Box makes sourcing materials a breeze.

Our chapters are organized by materials:
- Playing with Paper
- Playing with Paint
- Playing with Rolls
- Playing with Sticks
- Playing with Rocks
- Playing with Cardboard
- Playing with Yarn
- Playing with Fabric

Materials and Resources

The Handy Dandy Craft Box

The Handy Dandy Craft Box contains the basic materials necessary for making the crafts in this book, along with items for decorating your craft pieces.

Art and Craft for Elementary School

Other Materials

Recyclables

Materials and Resources

Other Resources

- Check out our website and join us on social media for other projects and updates on our events. You can also find out where to get our **Handy Dandy Craft Box**.

- Videos of all our projects can be seen on our DIY Place You Tube Channel
  https://www.youtube.com/channel/UCM_VQFNvvKxqzqLckjZMmNA

- www.diyplace.org

- Other platforms:

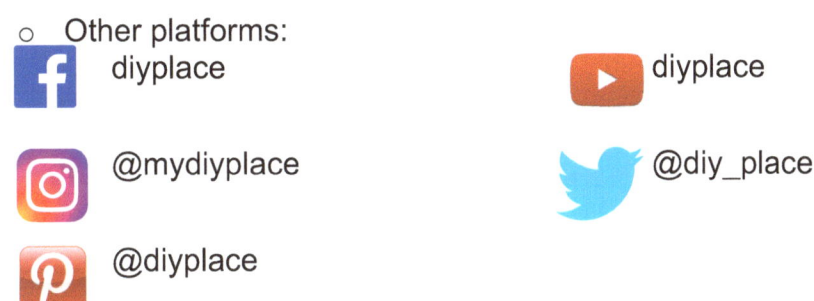

    diyplace   diyplace

    @mydiyplace   @diy_place

    @diyplace

Measurements

In this book, we use both imperial and metric measurements. For ease of use, all measurements are not converted exactly. Metric measurements are generally rounded up to the nearest whole number.

Art and Craft for Elementary School

How to Trace a Template

You can trace templates using either carbon paper, graphite or tracing paper. Both items are available in our Handy Dandy Craft Box.

Using Tracing Paper

Tracing paper is one of the easiest ways to trace a design or template because you can easily see what you are doing. Once your design is traced out, you can cut it out and use it many times over.

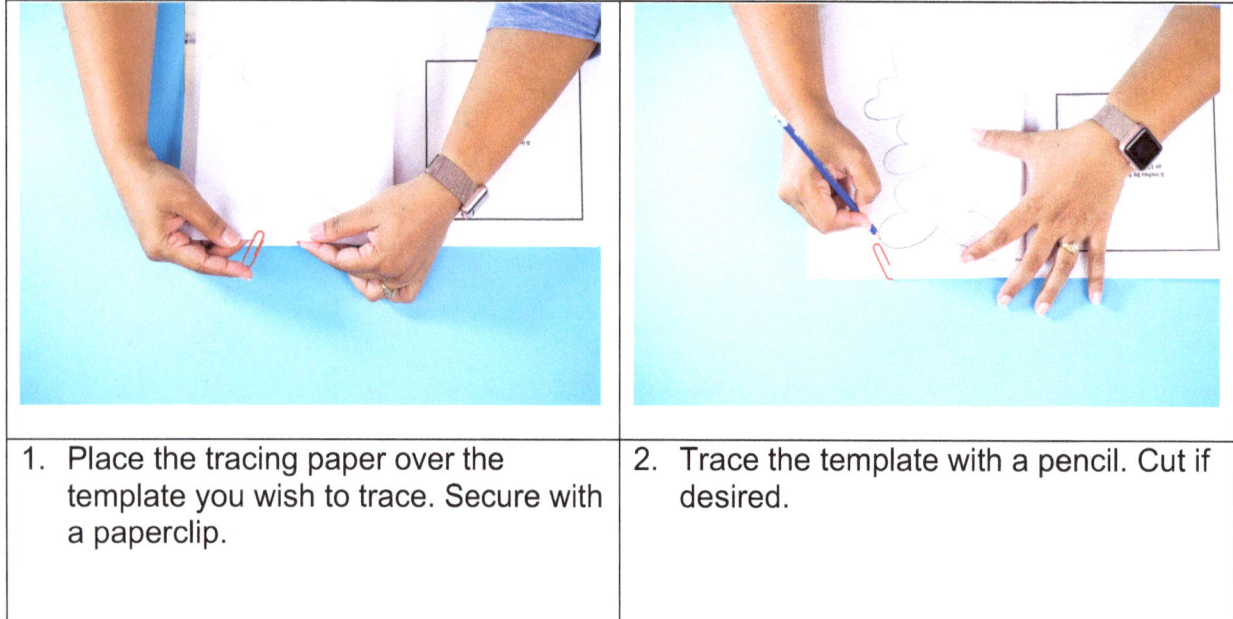

1. Place the tracing paper over the template you wish to trace. Secure with a paperclip.
2. Trace the template with a pencil. Cut if desired.

How to Trace from a Template

Using Carbon or Graphite Paper

Tracing with carbon or graphite paper is useful for many intricate designs and templates. It is especially useful to trace right onto your final paper. You can also trace your templates unto cardstock and cut them out. That way, you will have all your templates on hand to do your projects.

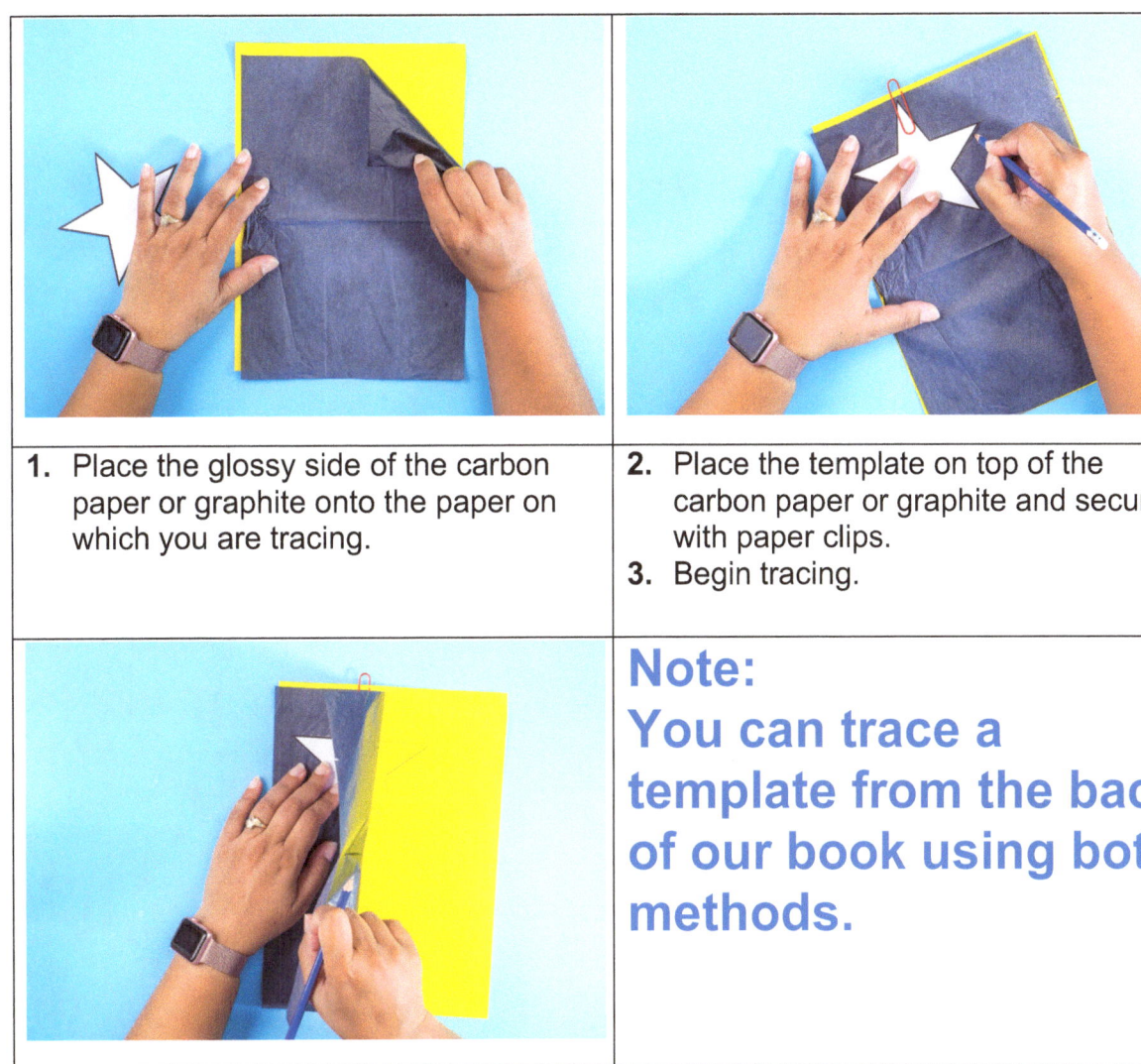

1. Place the glossy side of the carbon paper or graphite onto the paper on which you are tracing.

2. Place the template on top of the carbon paper or graphite and secure with paper clips.
3. Begin tracing.

3. Check to see that the whole image is traced before removing the template. Cut if desired.

Note: You can trace a template from the back of our book using both methods.

Playing with Paper

Paper is one of the easiest materials to source. You can purchase all kinds of paper, but did you know you can also get it free? Just look around – junk mail flyers, gift paper, packaging, old calendars and notebooks, are all great sources of paper. You can make some really fun items with paper.

In the section, "Playing with Paint", we show you how you can make your own patterned paper.

Playing with Paper

1. Nameplate

MATERIALS:

Craft Box
- Items for decorating

Recyclables and Other Materials and Tools
- One piece of white cardstock 8 ½" x 11" (use 22cm x 28cm)
- One piece coloured paper 2 ½" x 3" (use 6cm x 7cm)
- One piece coloured paper 2 ½" x 7" (use 6cm x 18cm)
- Marker
- One Photo 2" by 2 ½" (use 5cm x 6cm)
- Scissors

1. Fold the 8 ½" x 11" (22cm x 28cm) white cardstock in half on the long side.

2. Glue the coloured paper onto the name plate, as seen above. Write your name on the long piece of the coloured paper. Add your photo and decorate.

2 Idea Book

Art and Craft for Elementary School

MATERIALS:

Recyclables and Other Materials and Tools
1. One notebook
2. One piece patterned paper
3. Book template
4. Marker, scissors, clear tape

1. Open the book and place it onto the paper. Draw a 1" (3cm) border around the book and cut out the paper.

2. Place the book on the plain side of the paper. Fold the top and bottom into the inside cover of the book. Press firmly to secure.

3. Fold in and secure the other two ends of the book with clear tape.

4. Write your name on the book template. Cut out the book template and stick it onto the front of your book.

Playing with Paper

3. Caterpillar

MATERIALS:

Craft Box
- Two craft eyes.

Recyclables and Other Materials and Tools
- Five, 2" x 8 ½" (use 5cm x 22cm) strips of coloured paper
- Two, ¼" x 2" (use 1cm x 5cm) strips of coloured paper
- Scissors, glue and one black marker or pen

1. Form a circle with the red piece of paper and glue together

2. Place another strip of paper inside the first, form a circle and glue. Repeat steps until all five pieces are used.

3. Glue together the two, ¼" x 2" (1cm x 5cm) strips of cardstock to form a "V", for the caterpillar's antennae.

4. Glue the antennae and eyes, then draw a mouth on the caterpillar's head.

4 Pinwheel

MATERIALS:

Craft Box
- Decorative tape

Recyclables and Other Materials and Tools
- Patterned paper 6"x6" (15cm x 15cm)
- Pencil with an eraser
- One straight pin
- One pony bead
- Ruler
- Scissors

1. Draw an "X" connecting all the points of the paper.

2. Place a pencil mark on all four lines of the X, 1" (3cm) from the centre point.

3. Cut the paper from the four corners, only up to the pencil marks. Your paper should have four slits and eight tips.

4. Place a dot on each left tip. Push a pin through the dot, on one of the tips.

Playing with Paper

5. Push the pin through the other dots, then push the pin through the centre of the "X".

6. Carefully push the tip of the pin though the pony bead, then through the pencil's eraser.

7. Use the scissors to bend the pin along the side of the pencil.

8. Use decorative tape to secure the pin to the pencil. Make sure you cover the tip of the pin.

5. Folded Butterfly

MATERIALS:

Craft Box
- Half a chenille stem

Recyclables and Other Materials and Tools:
- Patterned paper e.g. gift paper, junk mail
- Square template
- Circle template
- Glue
- Scissors

1. Cut out a circle and a square from coloured paper using the templates

2. Glue the circle to one of the tips of the square.

3. Fold back and forth like a fan, all the way to the end, then fold in half.

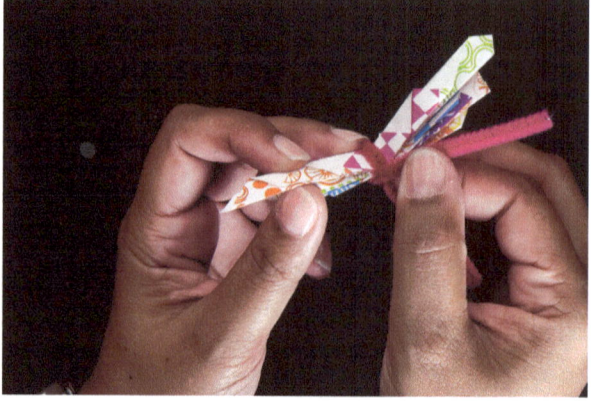

4. Wrap the chenille stem around the middle section of the butterfly. Curl the stem at the top to form the antennae. Open the butterfly's wings.

Playing with Paper

6. Basket

MATERIALS:

Craft Box
- Items for decorating

Recyclables and Other Materials and Tools
- One piece of 6" x 6" (15cm x 15cm) cardstock.
- One strip of ¾" x 6" (use 2cm x 15cm) cardstock
- Pencil
- Scissors
- Glue

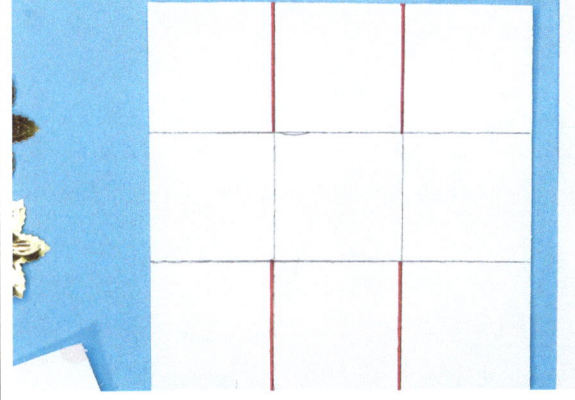

3. Draw two horizontal lines and two vertical lines 2" (5cm) apart, on the square cardstock, as shown above. Cut along the red lines.

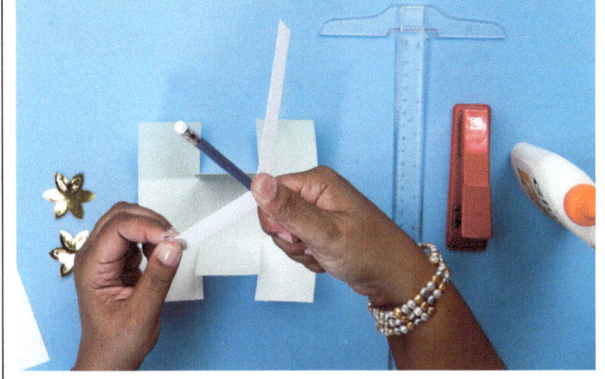

4. Use a pencil to curl the handle.

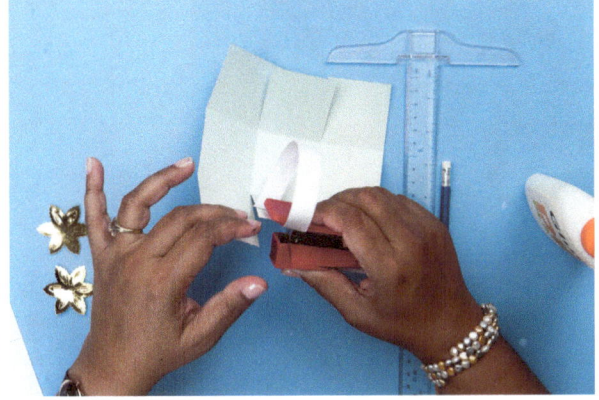

5. Attach the handle to the two centre pieces on the sides that were cut. You may use glue, or a stapler.

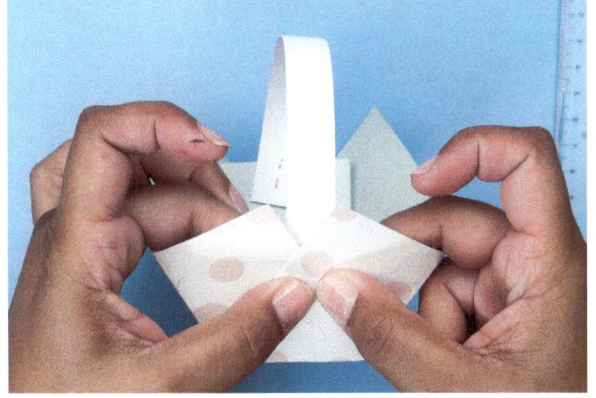

6. Bring up the two flaps to form a "V" at the handle. Glue the flaps to the handle. Decorate your basket.

Art and Craft for Elementary School

7. Banner 1

MATERIALS:

Craft Box
- Yarn

Recyclables and Other Materials and Tools
- Two pieces of 6" x 8" (15cm x 20cm) cardstock
- Ruler
- Pencil
- Scissors
- Paper punch

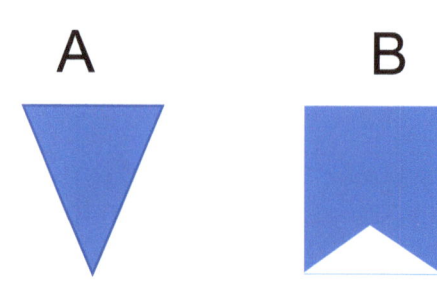

1. Banners A and B: Place a dot at the mid-point of the 6" (15cm) side. (This will be 3" (8cm) from either side)

2. Banner A: Join the points from the dot to the two tips of the paper and cut along the lines.

Playing with Paper

3. Banner B: Draw a line measuring 1 ½" (use 4cm) up from the 3" (8cm) point, as seen above. Connect the top of that line to the two bottom corners. Cut along the line.

4. Banners A and B: Punch a hole through each tip at the top of the banners.

5. Banners A and B: Run yarn, or string, through the holes

6. Decorate.

8 Banner 2

Art and Craft for Elementary School

MATERIALS:

Craft Box
- Yarn

Recyclables and Other Materials and Tools
- One sheet of kite or tissue paper per tassel
- Ruler
- Scissors
- Pencil

1. Fold the sheet of kite paper into four.

2. Measure 2" (5cm) from the folded area at the top. Draw a line across the top at that two inch mark. Draw lines from that top line to the bottom. These lines should be ½" (use 1cm) apart

Playing with Paper

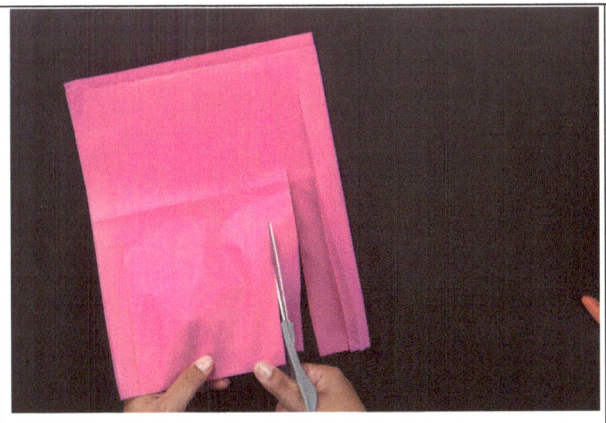

3. Cut along these lines as shown. Do not cut further than the first line drawn across the top.

4. Unfold your banner and pull together the middle portion.

5. Twist the middle of the banner

6. Place the twisted area over the yarn. Twist it again under the yarn to secure

9. Fan

MATERIALS:

Craft box
- One curvy fan stick
- Items for decorating

Recyclables and Other Materials and Tool
- Two pieces of cardstock 6"x 6" (15cm x 15 cm)
- Pencil
- Glue

1. Place a pencil mark 2" (5cm) from the top of the fan stick on both sides.

2. Add glue above the pencil mark.

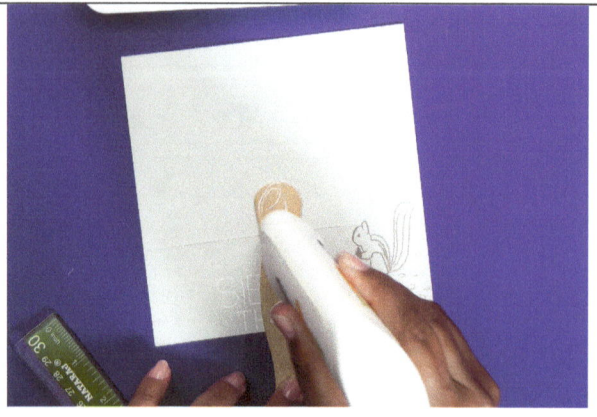

3. Place the side with glue on the back of one piece of the card stock, as seen above.

4. Add glue to the rest of the cardstock and place the other piece of cardstock over it. Decorate.

Playing with Paper

10. Simple Kite

MATERIALS:

Craft Box
- Two craft eyes
- 12 feet (use 3m) of yarn (or twine or thread)

Recyclables and Other Materials and Tools
- One sheet of paper approximately 8 ½" x 11" (use 22cm x 28cm)
- Glue, pen, pencil, scissors

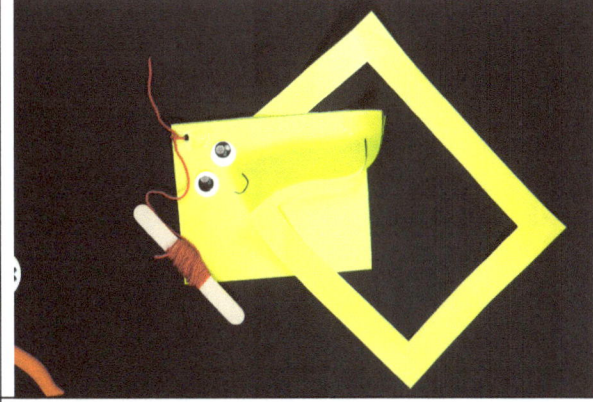

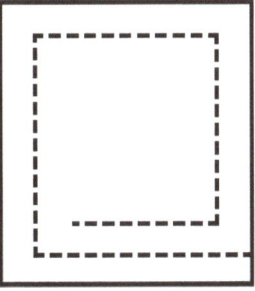

1. Draw lines on the paper, the width of your ruler, as shown above. Use the scissors and carefully cut along the dashed lines to make the kite's tail.

2. Place a piece of tape at the point where the kite's tail meets the body. Add eyes and a mouth, as shown above.

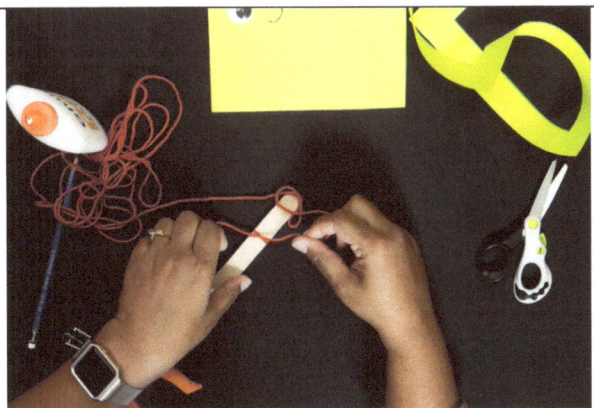

3. Cut a piece of yarn about 12' (use 3m) long or 5 arms' length. Wrap the yarn around a wooden craft stick.

4. Place a piece of tape in the top corner of the kite (above the eyes) and punch a hole through that corner. Tie your yarn through the hole. Your kite is ready to fly!

11. Heart Card

MATERIALS:

Craft Box
- Decorations
- Carbon paper

Recyclables and Other Materials and Tools
- One piece of 8½" x 11" (use 20cm x 28cm) white cardstock
- One piece of 6" x 6" (15cm x 15cm) red paper
- Large heart template
- Small heart template
- Pencil
- Scissors
- Paper clip
- Glue

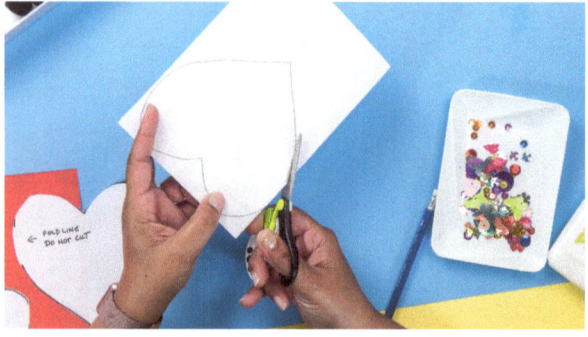

1. Fold the white cardstock in half and trace the large heart onto it. Cut out the card leaving part of the folded edge intact so it opens into a card

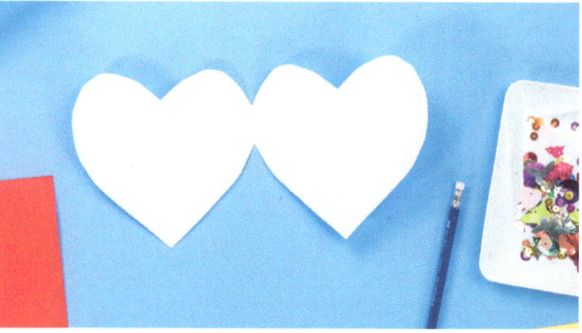

2. It opens into a card.

3. Trace the smaller heart onto the red paper and cut it out.
4. Fold the red heart in half and apply glue along the back fold.

5. Stick the red heart onto the front of the white heart card. Decorate.

Playing with Paper

12. Candle Card

MATERIALS: *Craft Box* o Decorations o Carbon paper *Recyclables and Other Materials and Tools* o One piece of 6" x 8" (15cm x 20cm) yellow cardstock o One piece of 6"x 6" (15cm x15cm) orange cardstock o One sheet of white cardstock (8 ½" x 11") (use 20cm x28cm) o Candle templates o Glue	
 1. Fold the white cardstock in half to form a card that is 8 ½" x 5" short (use 20 cm x 14 cm).	 2. Trace and cut the template for the candle base and flame, using two different colours.
 3. Glue the template onto the front of the card to form a candle. Decorate.	

13. Carnation Flower

MATERIALS:

Craft Box
- One chenille stem

Recyclables and Other Materials and Tools
- One sheet of tissue paper
- Scissors
- Paper clip
- Pencil
- Ruler

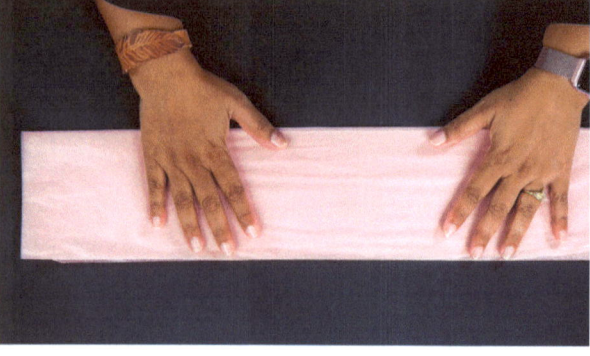

3. Fold your tissue paper into two on the long side. Fold again. You will now have four layers of tissue.

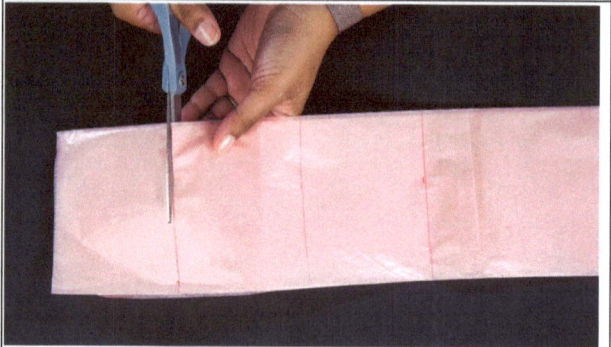

4. Measure and cut three pieces of 4" (10cm) strips, as seen above.

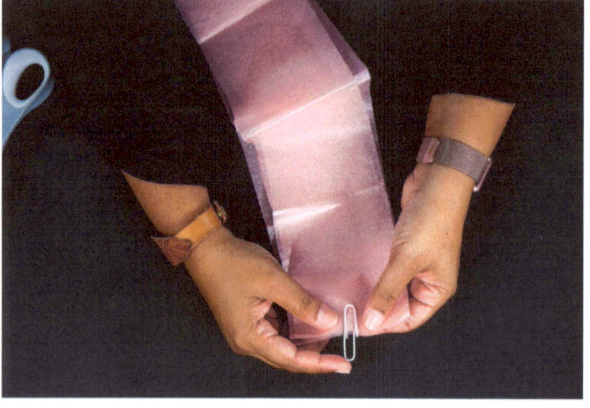

5. Unfold all the strips and lay them over each other. Hold the strips together with a paperclip on one end

6. Starting on the opposite end of the paper clip, fold the strips over and under to form a fan.

Playing with Paper

7. Tie the chenille stem around the middle of the fan and twist to secure

8. Carefully pull apart the layers of paper and fluff to shape the flower.

14. Jellyfish Sun Catcher

Art and Craft for Elementary School

Materials:

Craft Box
- Adhesive clear paper
- Ten, 10" (25cm) lengths of yarn. (You may use two colours)
- Strips of tissue paper
- Carbon paper

Recyclables and Other Materials and Tools
- Black cardstock
- Ruler
- Pencil
- Paper clip
- Scissors
- Jellyfish Sun Catcher frame template

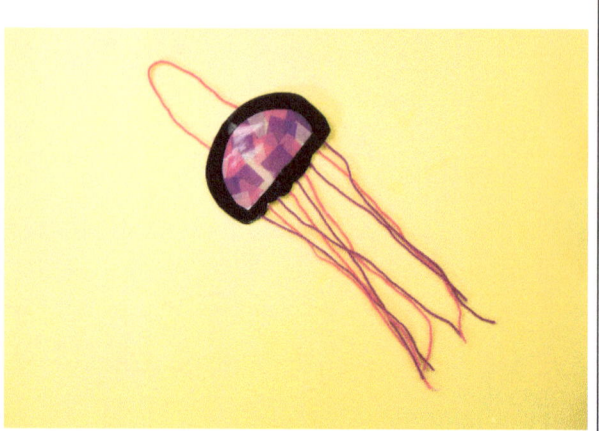

1. Trace and cut your Jellyfish Sun Catcher frame template using white cardstock. Use this template to trace and cut two Jellyfish Sun Catcher frames on black cardstock

2. Remove the backing from the clear adhesive and turn the sticky side to face upward. Stick one Jellyfish sun catcher frame onto the adhesive paper. Cut the excess adhesive paper from around the jellyfish sun catcher frame.

Playing with Paper

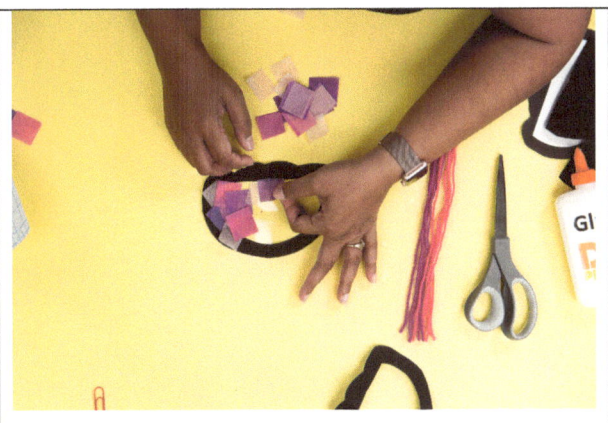
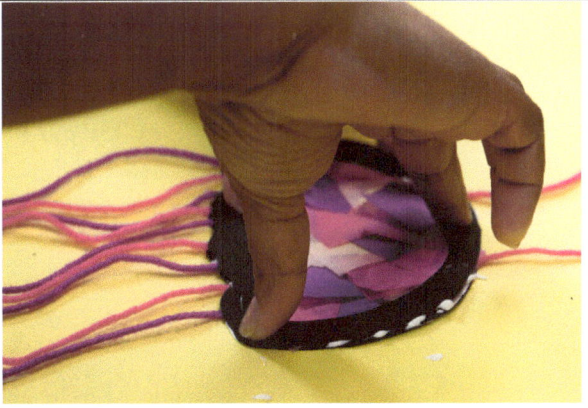

3. Cut the tissue strips into small squares and stick them on the adhesive paper in a random pattern.

4. Place glue at the bottom of the jellyfish frame and stick the strips of yarn to form tentacles. Loop and stick one strip of yarn at the top to create a handle.

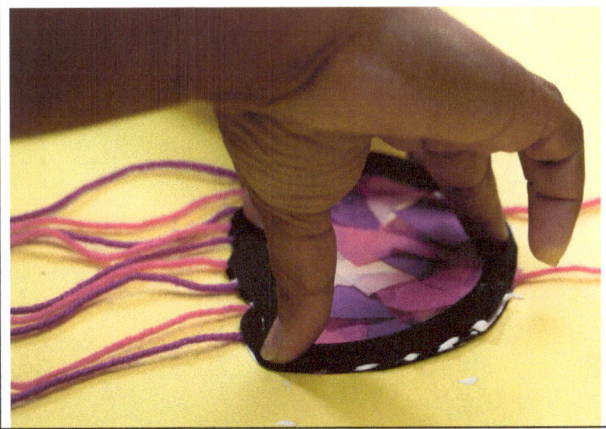

Cut any excess tissue paper that falls outside the frame.

5. Apply glue to the frame. Stick the second Jellyfish sun catcher frame over the first.

Playing with Paint

Paints and art can be used to teach the basics of design, including lines, colours, space, balance, texture, patterns and shapes. In this section, we explore some simple techniques. You can use these techniques to create your own patterned paper.

Playing with Paint

15. Patterns

MATERIALS:

Recyclables and Other Materials and Tools
- One sheet of sketch pad paper
- Paints (poster, tempera or acrylic)
- Paint brush
- Do It Yourself print stamps. e.g. a bottle cap; a paper roll; end of a celery stalk; a piece of bubble wrap placed around a box or a paper roll

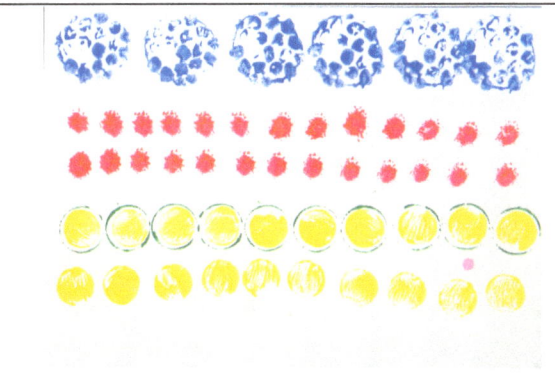

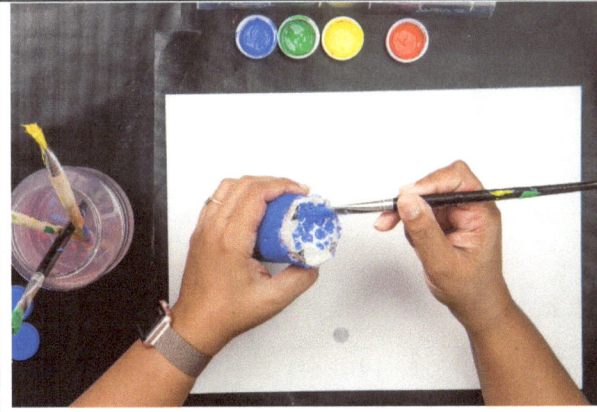

1. Dip your paint brush into any colour paint. Cover the rim of your DIY print stamp with the paint.

2. Place the bottle cap, paper roll, pom pom or other object onto the paper and press firmly.

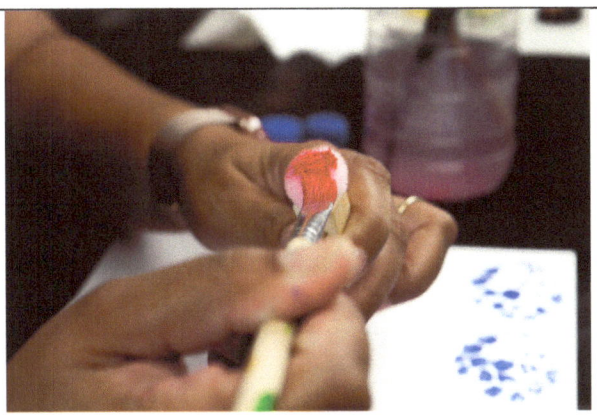

3. Repeat steps 1 and 2 until you are happy with your pattern. You can use the same stamp or another one.

16. Foam Stamping

MATERIALS:

Craft Box
- Foam sticker

Recyclables and Other Materials and Tools
- One sheet of sketch pad paper.
- Paints (poster, tempera or acrylic).
- Paint brush
- Bottle cap.

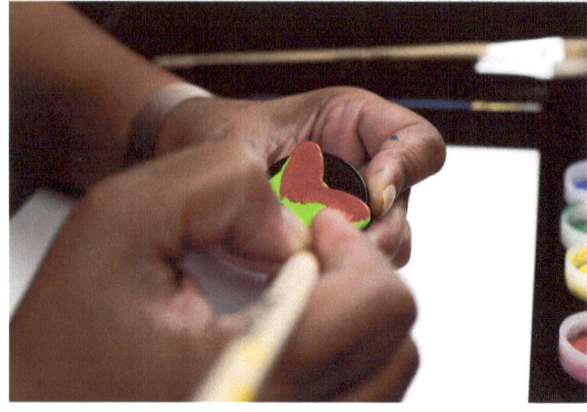

1. Make a stamp by sticking your foam sticker into the bottle cap

2. Dip your paint brush into any colour paint. Cover the foam stamp with paint.

3. Press the foam stamp onto the paper. Continue stamping until you are happy with your pattern

Playing with Paint

17. Blot Painting

MATERIALS:
Recyclables and Other Materials and Tools
   o One sheet of sketch pad paper.
   o Paints (poster, tempera or acrylic)
   o Paint brush

 1. Fold your paper in half.	 2. Add watery paint to your brush. Open your paper and place some blobs on the paper.
 3. Close the paper and swipe the paper with your hand to move the paint around. Open the paper.	 4. Repeat Steps two and three using different colours until you are happy with your pattern. What does your creation resemble?

18 Painting with Lines

Art and Craft for Elementary School

MATERIALS:

Recyclables and Other Materials and Tools
- One sketch pad page
- Paint (poster, acrylic or tempera)
- Paint brush
- Pencil
- Black marker

1. Draw big looped lines over your paper. (Take your pencil for a walk on the paper.)

2. Paint between the lines using different colours.

3. When the paint is dry, use your black marker to trace your pencil lines.
   What does your painting resemble?

32

Playing with Paper Rolls

Recyclable materials are great for making art and craft projects. Paper rolls are inexpensive and great for making many craft projects. Once you get started, you will realise that you can never have enough paper rolls!

19. How to cover a paper roll

1. Place your roll on the paper and measure to ensure the width of the paper can go around the roll. Measure the height of your roll and add one half inch at the top and bottom – (this is the height of your paper.) You can now cut your paper to this height.

2. Place glue on one end of the paper and attach the roll. Roll the paper around until you get to the other end

3. Add glue to the other end.

4. Tuck the top and bottom ends of the paper into the roll.

TIP - For a standard size roll you will need a piece of paper approximately 6" x 7" (15cm x 18 cm).

20. Butterfly Puppet

MATERIALS:

Craft Box
- One chenille stem
- Pair of craft eyes
- Decorations

Recyclables and Other Materials and Tools
- One tissue roll
- One piece of 6" x 7" (15 cm x 18cm) coloured paper
- One piece of 6" x 7" (15 cm x 18cm) white paper
- Butterfly template
- Black ink pen
- Tape
- Glue

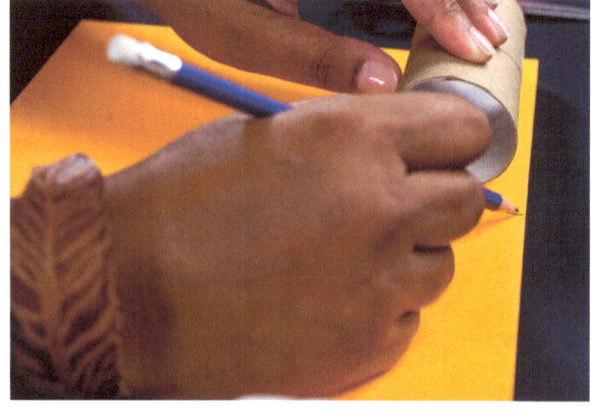

1. Cover the paper roll with your coloured paper, using the instructions at the start of this section.

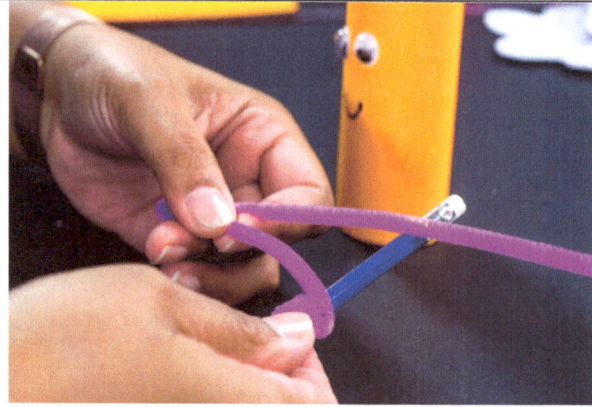

2. Fold the chenille stem into two. Roll the two tips of the stem over a pencil, to curl the butterfly's antennae and tape it into the roll.
Leave the antennae sticking out at the top.

Playing with Paper Rolls

3. Stick eyes on the butterfly and use your marker to draw on a smile.

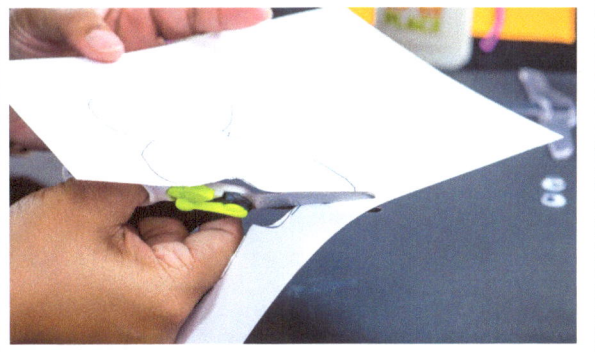

4. Trace and cut the butterfly template using the white paper (for the wings.)

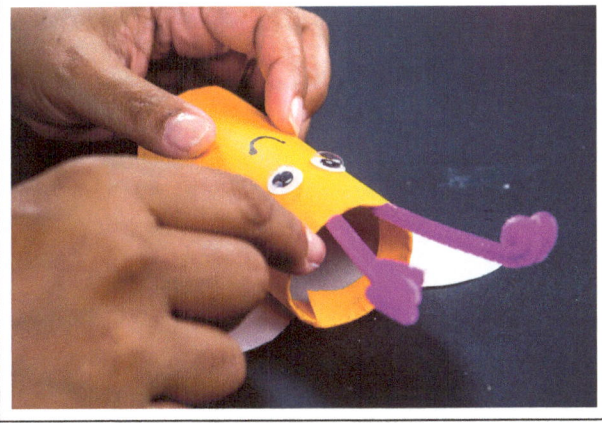

5. Glue the middle of the butterfly wing to the back of the roll and decorate.

6. Decorate your butterfly.

21. Bee Puppet

Art and Craft for Elementary School

MATERIALS:

Craft Box
- Two eyes
- Two black chenille stems

Recyclables and Other Materials and Tools
- Paper roll
- One piece of yellow paper approximately 6" x 7" (15cm x 18cm).
- One piece of white or black paper 6" x 6" (15 cm x15cm)
- Heart template
- Tape, scissors, glue and a black ink pen

1. Cover the paper roll with the yellow paper, using the instructions at the start of this section.

2. Roll one of the black chenille stems around the roll to form a spiral pattern. Secure with tape.

Playing with Paper Rolls

3. Use the top of the roll to trace and cut a yellow circle for the face. Add eyes and a mouth to the face.

4. Fold the other chenille stem into two. Roll the two tips of the stem over a pencil, to curl the bee's antennae and tape it into the roll. Leave the antennae sticking out at the top. Stick the bee's face on the roll.

5. Trace and cut the heart template using the white or black paper.

6. Tape the heart template to the back of the bee, to serve as its wings.

22. Robot Puppet

MATERIALS:

Craft Box
- One chenille stem
- Pom poms, beads or sequins
- Two craft eyes

Recyclables and Other Materials and Tools
- One tissue roll.
- One piece of 6" x 6" (15 cm x 15cm) foil.
- One piece of 6" x 6" (15 cm x 15cm) coloured paper
- Black pen or marker
- Glue

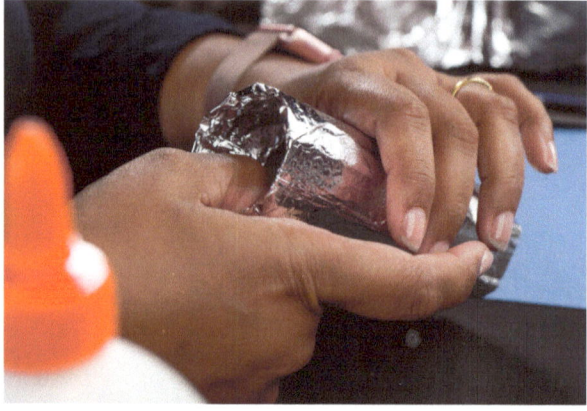

1. Cover the paper roll with foil, using the instructions at the start of this section.

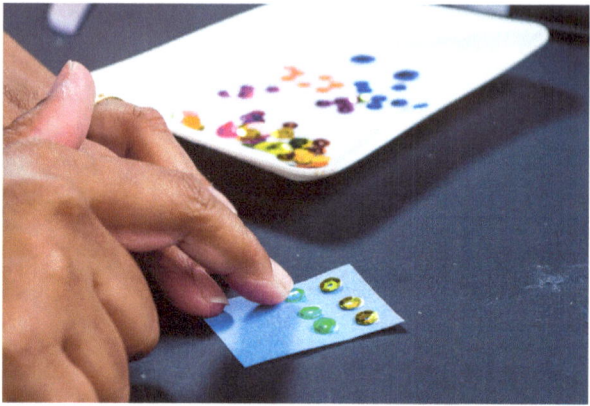

2. Cut a 2½" x 2" (use 6cm x 5cm) piece of paper for the body of the robot. Add "buttons" using pom poms, beads or sequins. Glue to the robot body

3. Glue the two eyes and add a mouth on the robot.

4. From the remaining paper, cut two strips to form arms. Fold the arms and glue to the body, as shown above.

Playing with Paper Rolls

23. Ninja Puppets

MATERIALS:

Craft Box
- One black or red chenille stem

Recyclables and Other Materials and Tools
- One coloured straw
- One tissue roll
- One piece of red or black paper approximately 6" x 7" (15cm x 18cm)
- One piece of narrow masking tape, 1" (3cm) long
- Black marker
- Glue

1. Cover the paper roll with red or black paper, using the instructions at the start of this section.

2. Place a piece of masking tape on the top area of the roll. Mark two eyes.

3. Cut a small strip of black paper for eye brows and glue these above the eyes.

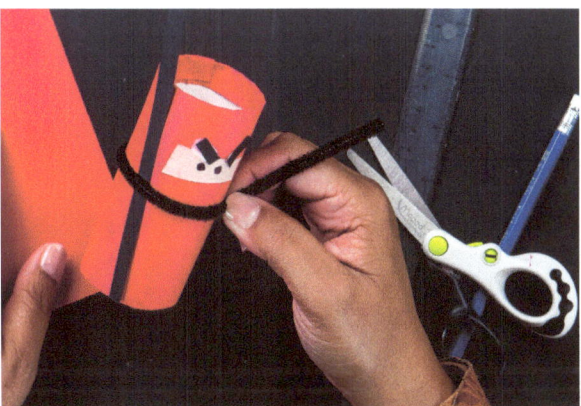

4. Use the chenille stem to attach the straw (or a thin strip of paper) to the body of the ninja puppet. Twist to secure.

24. Microphone

MATERIALS:

Craft Box
- One Styrofoam ball (or balled up paper)
- One red gem
- One green gem
- Other items for decorating

Recyclables and Other Materials and Tools
- One paper roll
- One piece of 6" x 7" (15cm x 18cm) coloured paper
- One piece of 12' x 12' (30cm x 30cm) foil paper
- Clear tape
- Decorative tape
- Ruler, scissors and glue

1. Cover the paper roll with coloured paper, using the instructions at the start of this section.

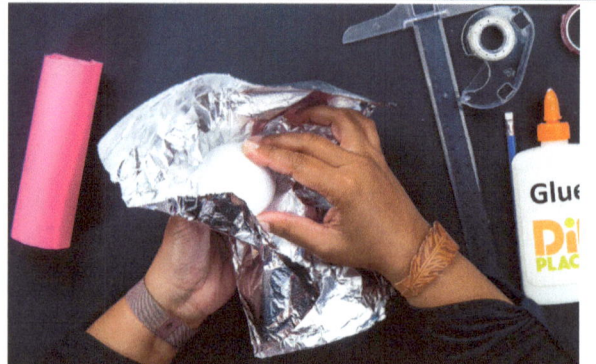

2. Cover your Styrofoam ball with the foil and twist at the bottom.

3. Place the ball into the roll and secure with tape.

4. Add an "On" and "Off" switch using gems. Decorate.

Playing with Paper Rolls

25. Lantern

MATERIALS:
Craft Box
   o Twelve inches of yarn
   o Pom poms or other decoration
Recyclables and Other Materials and Tools
   o One piece of coloured paper 6 ½" x 8" (use 16cm x 20cm)
   o Paper roll
   o Paper punch
   o Pencil,
   o Scissors
   o Glue

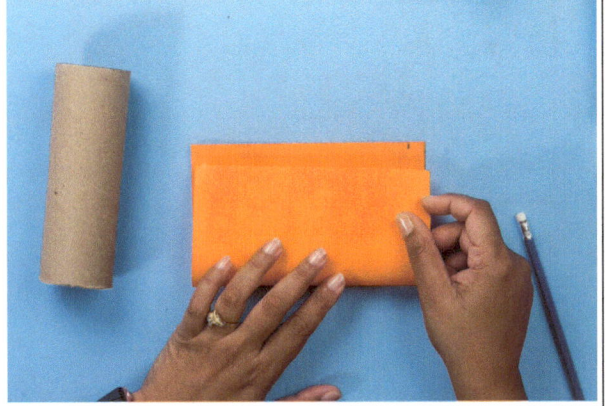 1. Fold the paper in half. The two narrow sides must measure 4" (10cm). The two wide sides must measure 6 ½" (use 16cm).	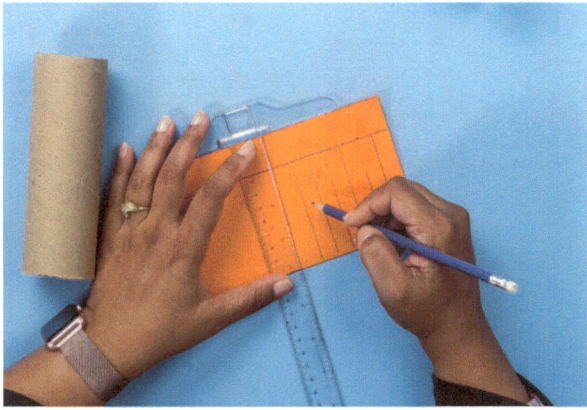 2. Draw a line one inch from the top of the wide side. (not the side with the fold) Using a ruler and pencil, draw ten lines as seen above. Cut the ten lines.
 3. Open the paper. Glue the top and bottom of the paper to the top and bottom of the roll. (The middle of the paper will "stick out" to form the lantern)	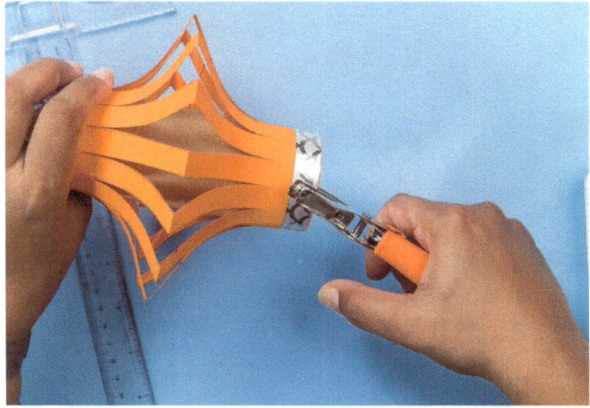 4. Punch two holes at the top and tie the string or yarn for hanging. Decorate.

26. Paper Village

MATERIALS:

Recyclables and Other Materials and Tools

- Paper roll
- One piece of coloured paper to cover the roll
- One piece of coloured paper to create a roof for the house
- Once piece of coloured paper for the door and windows,
- One piece of firm cardboard 18"x14" (use 46cm x 36cm)
- Glue
- Markers
- Scissors

1. Cover the paper roll with coloured paper, using the instructions at the start of this section.

2. Measure a piece of paper for the roof by folding it in half to from a peak in the middle. Draw lines or patterns on the roof paper.

Playing with Paper Rolls

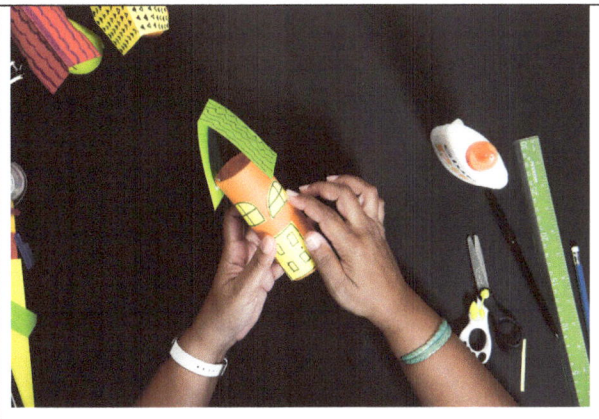

3. Draw a door and windows on pieces of coloured paper and cut them out.

4. Glue the roof, door and windows to the roll.

NOTE: You can create an entire village! You may even choose to get creative and add trees, children and other interesting things to your village.

You can make modern or ancient cities.

Complete your village with a fire house, a police station, a library etc.

27. Rainmaker

Art and Craft for Elementary School

MATERIALS:	
Craft Box o Yarn o Items for decorating *Recyclables and Other Materials and Tools* o One long paper roll o One piece of plain or coloured paper 12" x 8" (30cm x 20cm) o Two pieces brown paper each 5" x 5" (13 cm x 13cm) o Quarter cup of rice o Scissors o Glue	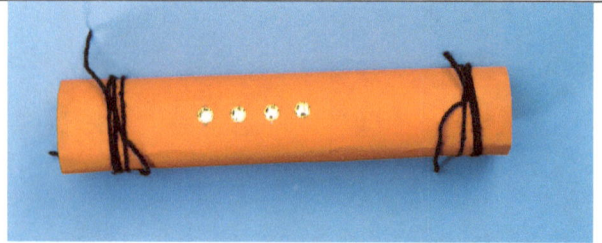

1. Use the tape to stick one piece of brown paper at one end of the roll.

2. Pour rice into the roll and stick the other piece of brown paper over the open end.

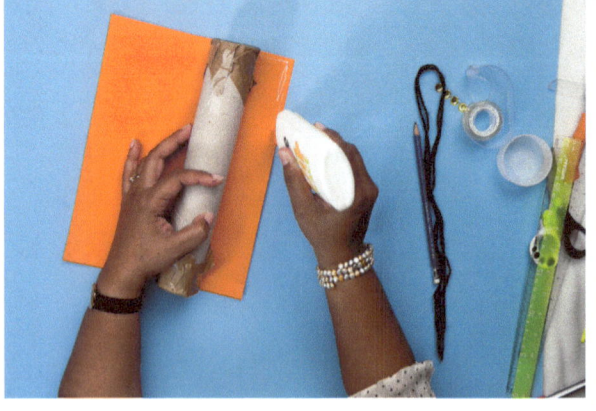

3. Cover the paper roll with coloured paper, using the instructions at the start of this section.

4. Decorate with yarn at both ends and decorate with gems or spangle as shown above.

Playing with Sticks

Craft sticks (or lolly sticks) can be used to make a variety of crafts. In this section, we learn how use sticks to make easy crafts. The techniques developed here can be used to create more complex designs.

28. Pencil Bookmark

MATERIALS: *Craft Box* ○ Large craft stick 8" (20cm) long *Recyclables and Other Materials and Tools* ○ Markers (pink, grey and yellow) ○ Black ink pen	
	3. Use the pink marker to colour one of the ends of the stick to create an "eraser". 4. Use the grey marker to colour a small strip of grey just below the pink area. This grey strip represents the metal part of your pencil.
1. Measure and mark off one inch from both ends of the stick.	

3. Use the yellow marker to colour the body of your pencil bookmark.	4. On the other end of the stick, use the black pen to draw the pencil tip. Write your name and repeat on the other side.

29. Foam Sticker Bookmark

MATERIALS:

Craft Box
- Large craft stick
- Two foam stickers
- Craft eyes
- Glitter glue

1. Stick the foam stickers onto the top of each side of the craft stick.

2. Stick the eyes on the foam sticker and draw a smile. Decorate.

Playing with Sticks

30. Critter Bookmark

MATERIALS:

Craft Box
- One Jumbo craft stick 8" (20cm) long
- One large pom pom
- Two craft eyes
- Glitter glue
- Decorations

Recyclables and Other Materials and Tools
- Glue

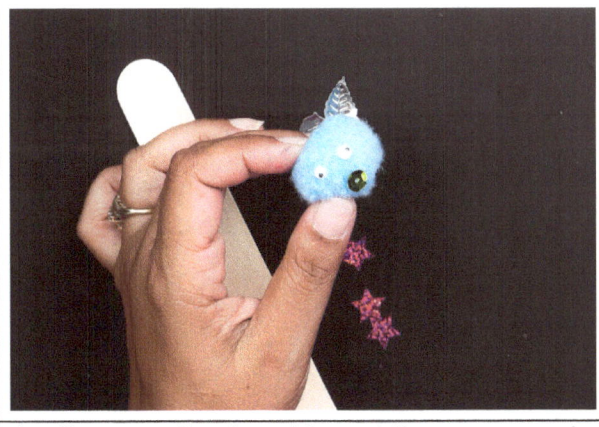

1. Prepare the head by adding eyes and a sequin for a mouth to the pom pom.

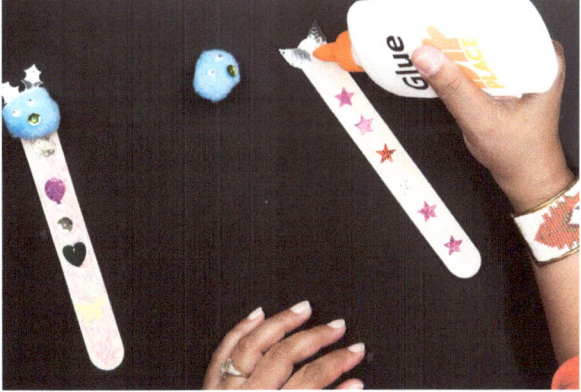

2. Add "ears" to the stick. Glue the head onto the top of the stick and decorate.

31. Airplane

MATERIALS:

Craft Box
- 4 Craft sticks
- 1 Clothespin
- Decorations

Recyclables and Other Materials and Tools
- Markers
- Glue

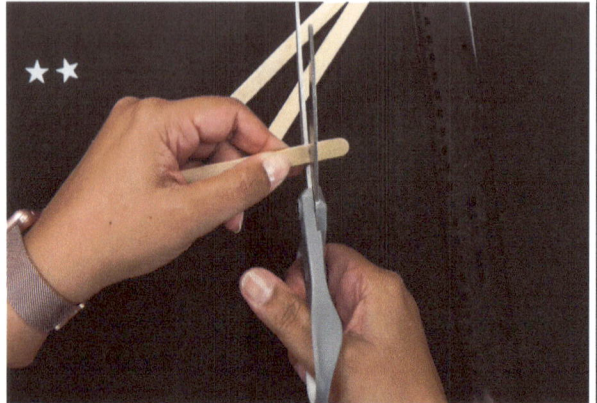

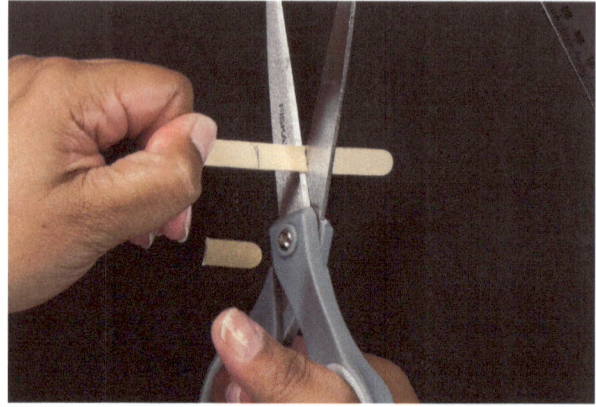

1. Cut one inch off the edge of one craft stick

   (You will have one short piece for the top of the tail wing and the long piece for the base of the tail wing.)

2. For the tail wing, place the small piece you just cut in the middle of another craft stick and measure. Mark the lines and cut both ends, as shown above.
   (These go on top the base of the tail wing).
   Discard the middle piece.

3. Colour and decorate your sticks.

4. Glue two long sticks above and below the front of the clothespin for the front wings. Glue the long piece from (1) to the top back of the clothespin.

5. Glue the three pieces onto the back tail with the Short piece from (1) sticking up in the middle, as shown above and the two pieces from (2) on either side.

Playing with Sticks

32. Pencil Topper

MATERIALS:

Craft Box
- One chenille stem,
- Two craft eyes

Recyclables and Other Materials and Tools
- Small pom pom
- Two pencils

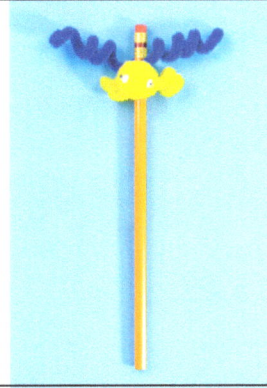

1. Find the midpoint of the chenille stem and wrap it around the top of the pencil. Twist to secure it.

2. Use another pencil or pen to roll the top of each side of the chenille stem. (You may add more than one stem.)

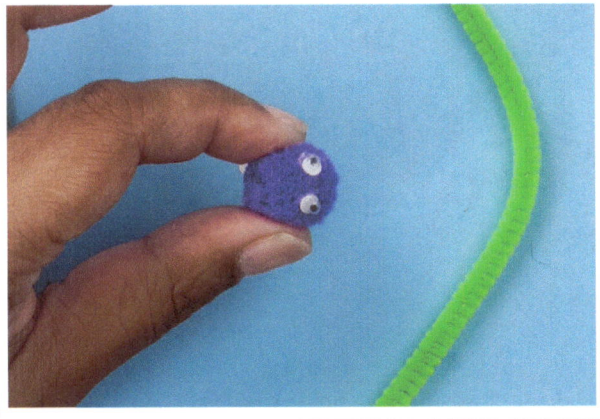

3. Glue the eyes onto the pom pom.

4. Place glue in the middle of the chenille stem. Stick the pom pom onto the chenille stem.

33. Picture Frame

MATERIALS:

Craft Box
- 15 craft sticks
- One strip magnet 3" (8 cm)
- Pom poms or other decorations

Recyclables and Other Materials and Tools
- Picture 2" by 2" (5cm x 5cm)
- Glue

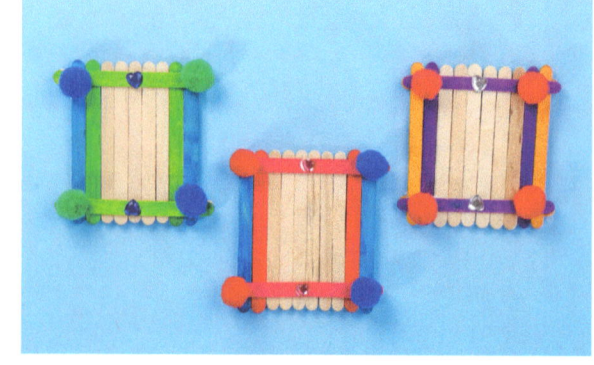

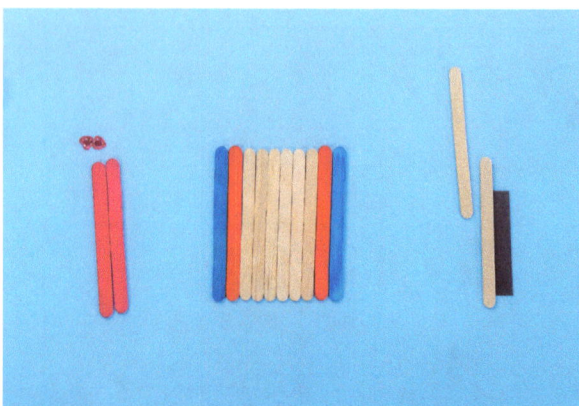

1. Place ten craft sticks side by side to form a base. You may also use coloured sticks also.

2. Place glue on three craft sticks and place them on the base, as shown above. Add the adhesive magnet strip to the diagonal piece, as shown above.

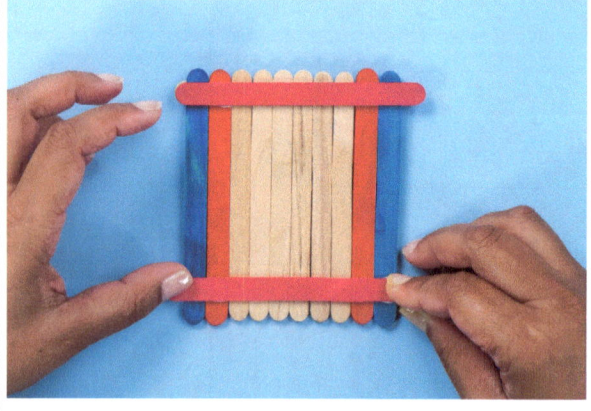

3. Turn it over and add two more craft sticks to the top and bottom of the base, as shown above.

4. Decorate and add a photo.

Playing with Sticks

34. Tree

MATERIALS: *Craft Box* o 8 craft sticks of one colour o 1 craft stick of a different colour o One star o Items for decorating *Recyclables and Other Materials and Tools* o Glue	
 1. Make a triangle with three of the same coloured sticks. Glue them together.	 2. Glue one craft stick from the top point of the triangle to the bottom, as seen above.
 3. Add the other craft sticks from the top point to the bottom, to cover empty spaces.	 4. Glue the final stick at the bottom of your tree to form the trunk. Decorate as desired.

35. House Magnet

MATERIALS:

Craft Box
- 16 Craft sticks
- One Magnet strip
- Items for decorating
- Foam stickers
- Glitter glue

Recyclables and Other Materials and Tools
- Glue

1. Place nine craft sticks side by side to form a base. Place glue on two craft sticks and place them on the base and the top as shown above. Let dry and turn over.

2. Glue the tips of two sticks to the top of the base to form a roof. Place another stick over these two stick (as seen above) to secure it in place.

3. Decorate the front.

4. Add two ticks to the top and the base of the back. Add the magnet strip to the stick at the top.

Playing with Sticks

36. Pencil Holder

MATERIALS:

Craft Box
- 24 craft sticks
- 1 Chenille Stem

Recyclables and Other Materials and Tools
- 1 can (washed with the label removed)
- Rubber band
- Glue

1. Line up your sticks in the order you want them to be placed on your can.

2. Place glue on one craft stick and adhere it to the side of the can. Place the rubber band around the can and the stick.

3. Continue gluing sticks around the can, placing them under the rubber band. Leave it to dry.

4. Remove the rubber band and wrap a chenille stem around to keep secure. Twist the two ends of the chenille stem to keep it in place.

Playing with Rocks

In most cases, rocks and pebbles are readily available, making crafts very inexpensive.
In some cases, where the correct size and shape of rocks cannot be easily found, we suggest using clay as an alternative (for example - in the Dominoes craft).

37. Painted Rocks

MATERIALS:

Recyclables and Other Materials and Tools
- One Rock (or rock alternative)
- Paints (acrylic, poster or tempera paint)
- Paintbrushes – one medium, one small
- Glue and water

Choose inspirational quote, saying or word, that can fit on your rock.

1. Paint your rock in a base colour. You may need two coats of paint. Leave to dry

2. Using your small paint brush, paint an inspirational quote and then decorate around your quote.

3. Once dry, apply a thin coat of glue and water. Leave to dry.

Playing with Rocks

38. Dominoes

MATERIALS: *Recyclables and Other Materials and Tools* o Rocks or shaped clay o Black and white paint o Paintbrushes – one medium, one small	
 1. Paint your rock or shaped clay black and leave to dry. You may need two coats of paint.	 2. Using the small brush and white paint, paint a line across the middle of the rock.
 3. Add dots to represent domino pieces (numbers 0 to six).	Note: If you cannot find appropriate rocks, you may make your own, using clay.

55

39. Tic Tac Toe Game (1)

MATERIALS:

Recyclables and Other Materials and Tools
- Burlap or other small bag or
- One 6"x 6" (15cm x 15cm) piece of paper, felt, fabric
- 10 round rocks or shaped clay about 1" (use 3cm) wide
- Ruler
- Black Marker

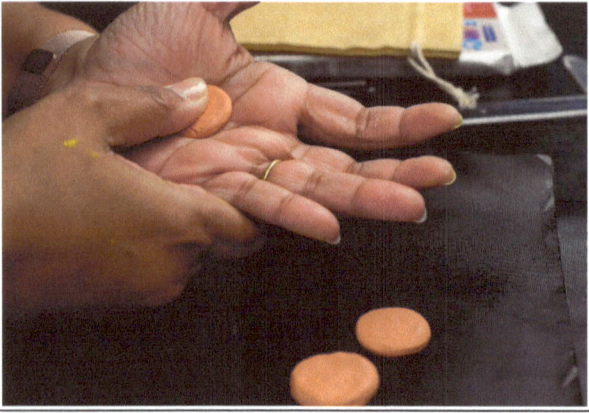

1. Choose your rocks or shape your clay and leave to dry.

2. Draw a grid on your burlap bag (or paper, felt, fabric), as shown above.

3. Draw "O"s and "X"s on your rocks or clay pieces (five pieces each).

Have fun!

Art and Craft for Elementary School

Playing with Rocks

40. Rock Frame

MATERIALS:

Recyclables and Other Materials and Tools
- One piece stiff cardboard
- One piece soft cardboard
- One piece black cardstock
  All 5" x 7" (use 13 cm x 18 cm)
- One strip soft cardboard
  5" x 1" (use 12 cm x 3cm)
- Pebbles and a seashell (optional)
- Glue

1. Fold the soft 5" x 7" (use 12cm x 17cm) cardboard into two and place glue on the top half as seen above.
2. Adhere the top half to the stiff cardboard.

3. Bend the strip at 1" (use 3cm) on each side. Attach one side to the bottom of the soft cardboard.
   (It will be between the soft cardboard and the stiff cardboard)

4. Adhere the black cardstock to the front of the stiff cardboard. Using glue stick the pebbles around the frame of the black piece. Let dry.

5. Turn over and attach the other side of the strip to the stiff cardboard as shown. This will allow your frame to stand.

Art and Craft for Elementary School

Playing with Cardboard

Cardboard can be found in many places: discarded packaging such as cereal boxes, packing boxes; the back of a used notepad or sketchbook; packaging for toys and other items.

41. Magazine / Book Holder

MATERIALS:

Recyclables and Other Materials and Tools
- Small cereal box
- Wrapping paper
- Scissors
- Pencil
- Ruler
- Clear tape / glue or glue stick

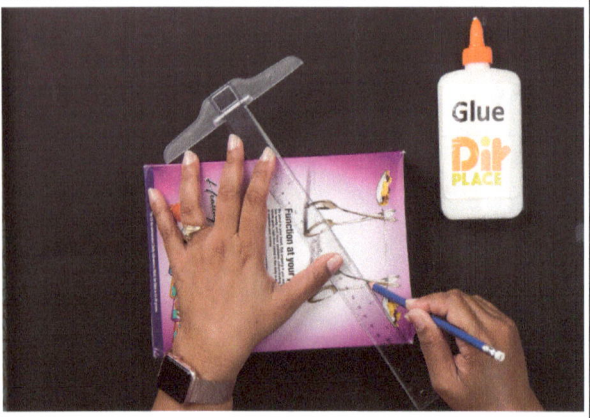

1. Start by drawing a diagonal line from the top right corner of the box, to the middle left as shown above.
2. Continue this line around the box and with another diagonal line (from left to right) on the other side.

3. Cut along the marked lines.

Playing with Cardboard

3. Measure a piece of gift or wrapping paper. Ensure it is at least 2" (use 5cm) longer than the height of the box. It should be able to wrap around the box leaving a 1" (use 3cm) excess

4. Glue one side of the box on the wrapping paper. Let dry.
5. Draw a line 1" (use 3cm) above the top of the box as shown above. Do this for the front and back of the box.
6. Cut off the excess paper.

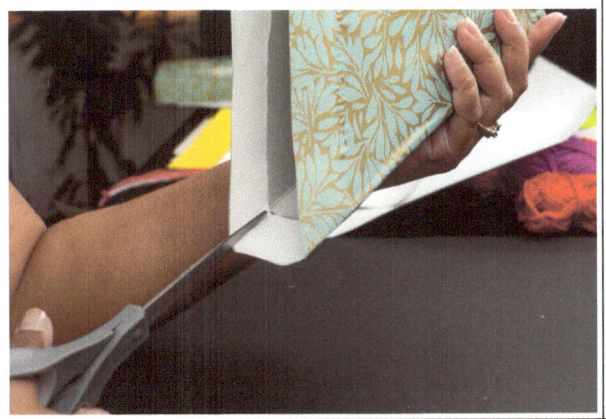

5. Glue the wrapping paper around the box.
6. Cut 1" (use 3cm) into the corners at the top being careful not to cut the box.
7. Glue and press all loose ends into the box.

8. Fold in and glue the flaps at the bottom of the box.

42. Card/Paper Holder

Art and Craft for Elementary School

MATERIALS:

Recyclables and Other Materials and Tools
- One small box
- Wrapping paper sufficient to cover the box
- Scissors
- Pencil
- Ruler
- Clear tape / glue or glue stick

1. Cut off the top flaps of the box.

2. Measure a piece of gift or wrapping paper. Ensure it is at least 2" (use 5cm) longer than the height of the box. It should also be able to wrap around the box. Fold 1" (use 3cm) at the bottom.

3. Glue the wrapping paper around the box. Cut 1" (use 3cm) into the corners at the top being careful not to cut the box.

4. Glue and press all loose ends into the box.

Playing with Cardboard

43. Star Door Hanger

MATERIALS:

Craft Box
- One 24" (use 61cm) length of yarn

Recyclables and Other Materials and Tools
- Patterned cardstock
- Star template
- Scissors
- Pencil
- Glue

1. Trace and cut six star templates from the cardstock.

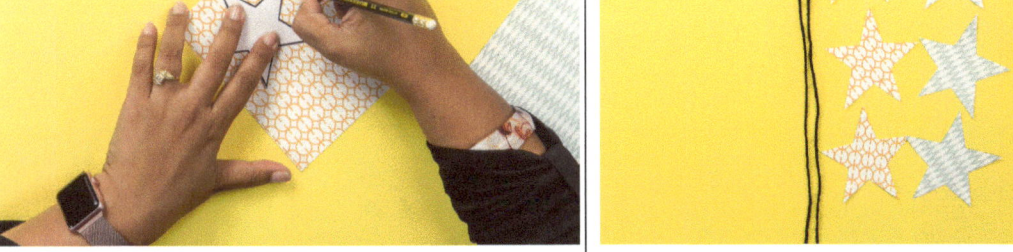

2. Form a row of three stars

3. Fold the yarn in half and glue it onto the back of a row of three stars. Leave a loop on top.

4. Glue the other three stars on top of the first set, as seen above. Leave to dry.

44. Butterfly Mobile

MATERIALS:

Craft Box
- Five pieces of yarn as follows:
  - 24", 21", 18", 15" and 12"
  - or use 61cm, 53cm, 46cm, 38cm and 30cm

Recyclables and Other Materials and Tools
- Cardstock (patterned on both sides)
- Butterfly template
- Two pieces of 4 ½" x 6" (use 11x 15cm) plain coloured paper
- Two pieces of 2" x 5" (5cm x 13cm) cardboard
- Glue
- Pencil
- Hole punch

1. Trace and cut four butterfly templates from the cardstock.

2. Place a piece of clear tape down the middle of each of your butterflies. Trim off any excess tape. Punch a hole at the top middle of each butterfly.

Playing with Cardboard

3. Cover the front and back of the two pieces of cardboard with the two pieces of 4 ½" x 6" (use 11x 15cm) plain coloured paper. Glue the two pieces of cardboard together to form an "X" Punch holes at each of the four ends.

4. Place the longest piece of yarn through the hole of one butterfly then through one hole of the "X".

5. Repeat steps four and five with the remaining butterflies.

1. Attach the last piece of yarn to 2 opposite holes on the "X" to form a handle.

Playing with Yarn

In our projects, we use a lot of yarn because a ball of yarn can go a long way in making crafts. Alternatives to yarn can include string, curling ribbon, satin ribbon, thread, lace and stripped fabric.

45. Tassels

MATERIALS:

Craft Box
- Two 12" (30cm) pieces of yarn
- One 20' (use 6m) piece of yarn (your choice of colour)

Recyclables and Other Materials and Tools
- One piece of cardboard 4" x 3" (10cm x 8cm)
- Scissors

1. Place one short piece of yarn on the short side of the cardboard and secure it with tape, as seen above.

2. Wrap the other longer piece of yarn around the long side of the cardboard at least fifty times.

Playing with Yarn

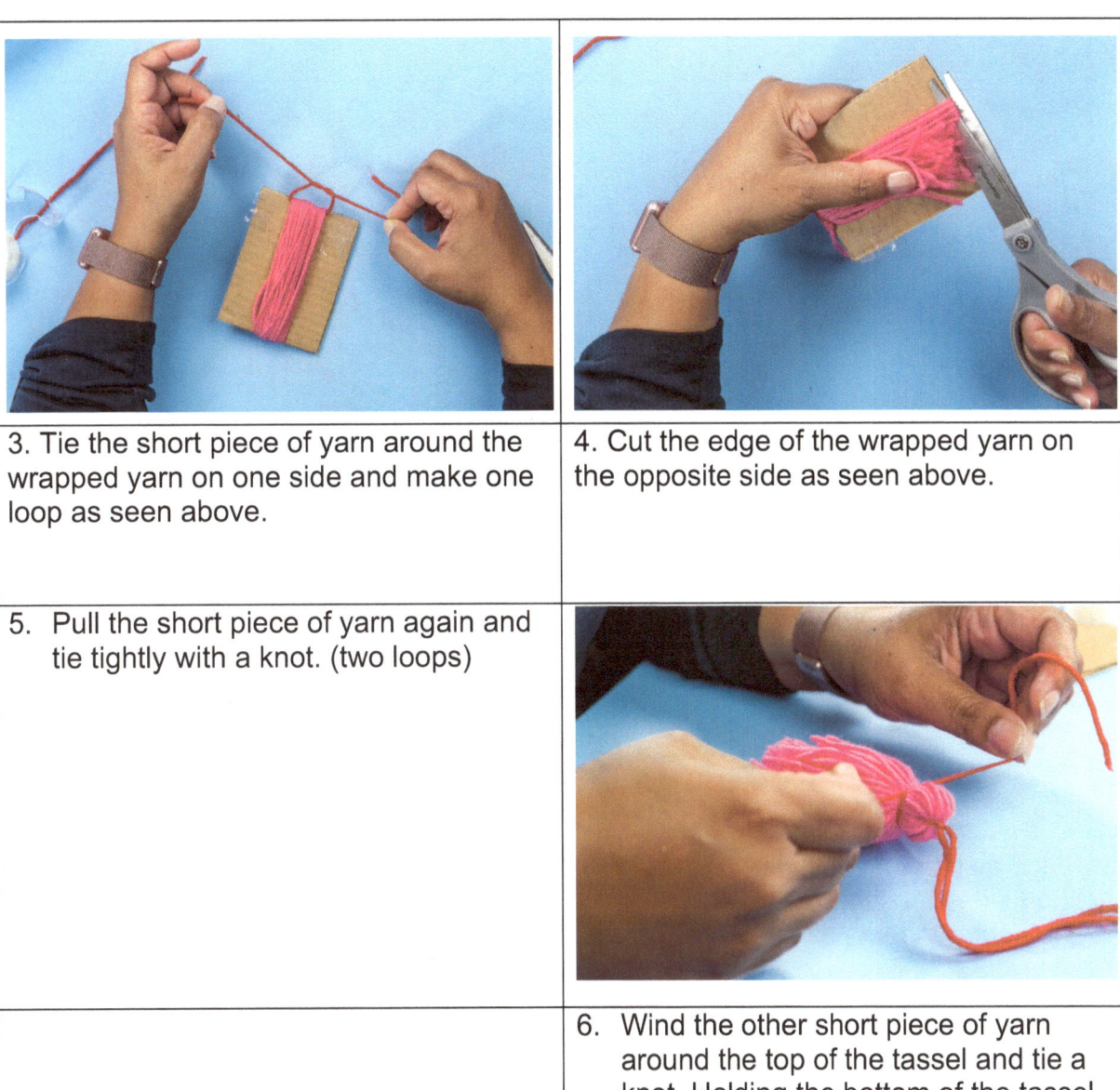

3. Tie the short piece of yarn around the wrapped yarn on one side and make one loop as seen above.

4. Cut the edge of the wrapped yarn on the opposite side as seen above.

5. Pull the short piece of yarn again and tie tightly with a knot. (two loops)

6. Wind the other short piece of yarn around the top of the tassel and tie a knot. Holding the bottom of the tassel between your fingers, trim to even the bottom.

46. Pom Poms

MATERIALS:

Craft Box
- One 12" (30cm) piece of yarn
- One 3' (use 91cm) piece of yarn (your choice of colour)

Recyclables and Other Materials and Tools
- One piece of 1" x 2 ½ " (use 3cm x 6cm) cardboard
- Clear tape
- Scissors

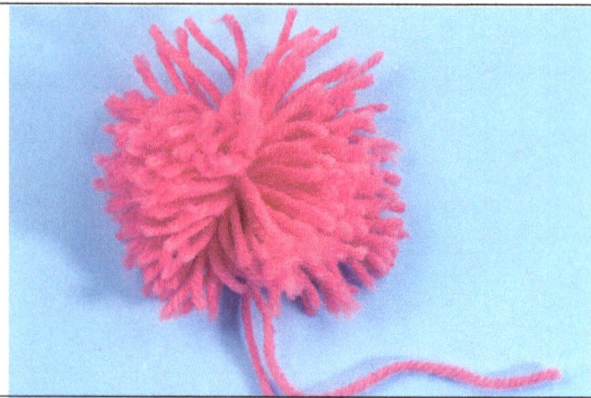

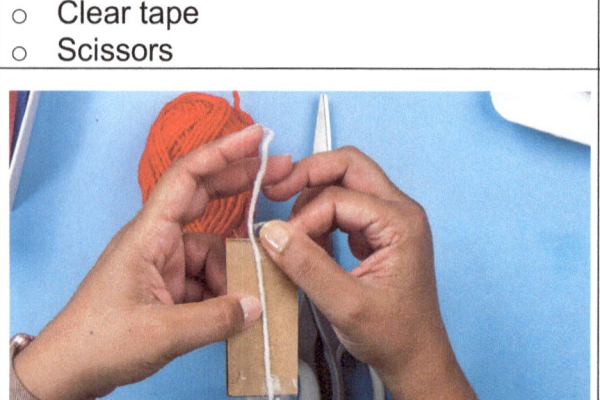

1. Place a short piece of yarn on the short side of the cardboard and secure it with tape, as seen above.

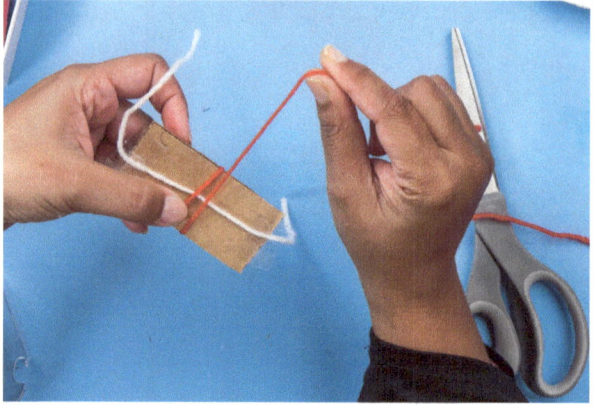

2. Wrap the longer piece of yarn around the long side of the cardboard at least twenty five times.

3. Pull the short piece of yarn around the wrapped yarn on one side and make only one loop.

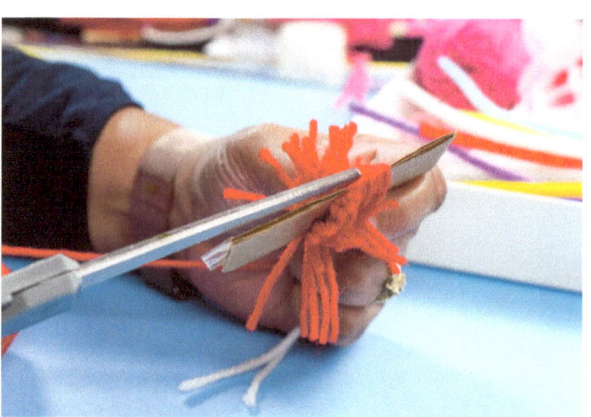

4. Cut the edge of the wrapped yarn on the opposite side. Pull the short end of the yarn and tie tightly with two knots.

Playing with Yarn

47. Ninja Star

MATERIALS:	
Craft Box ○ Three lengths of coloured yarn (3 colours) each 3' (use 1m) *Recyclables and Other Materials and Tools* ○ One piece of soft cardboard (5" x 5" or 13cm x 13 cm) ○ Two pieces of coloured paper (5" x 5" or 13cm x 13 cm) ○ Star Template ○ Pencil ○ Scissors ○ Glue	
 2. Trace the star template onto the cardboard and two pieced of colored paper and cut them out. Stick a coloured star on either side of the cardboard.	 3. Tie the end of one piece of yarn around one of the star points.
	4. Wrap the yarn around each point of the star ten times until you return to the point where you started. Tie the two ends of the yarn to form a knot and trim. 5. Repeat step 3 with the two other colours of yarn. 6. Decorate.

48 Friendship Bracelet

Art and Craft for Elementary School

MATERIALS

Craft Box
- Six pieces of yarn 14" (36 cm) long.

Recyclables and Other Materials and Tools
- One strip of 11" (28cm) paper
- Tape
- Scissors

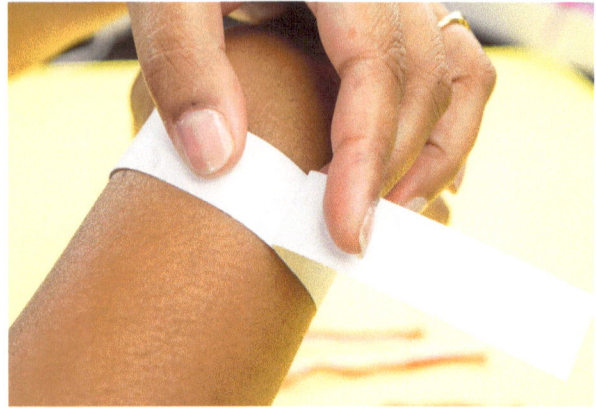

1. Measure the paper around your wrist. Add an extra 3" (7cm) to the length of the paper – this will be the length of your bracelet

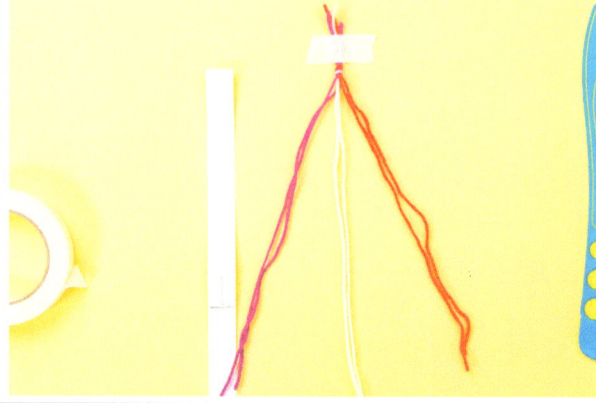

2. Tie a knot at the top of the 6 pieces of yarn.
3. Secure the knot on your work surface with tape and place the paper measure alongside.

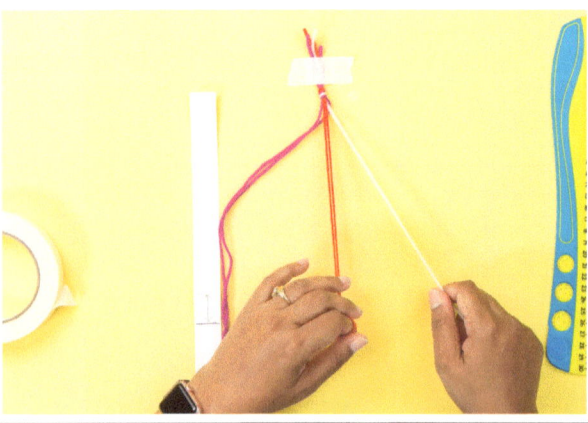

4. Separate the yarn into three pieces.
5. Braid the yarn in the following fashion:
   A. Bring the right piece to the centre and move the centre piece to the right.

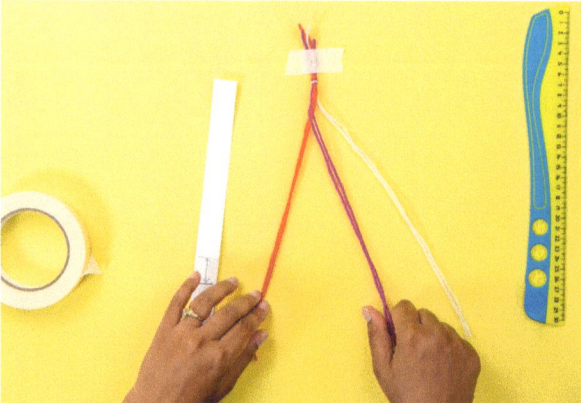

6. B. Bring the left piece to the centre and move the centre piece to the left.

68

Playing with Yarn

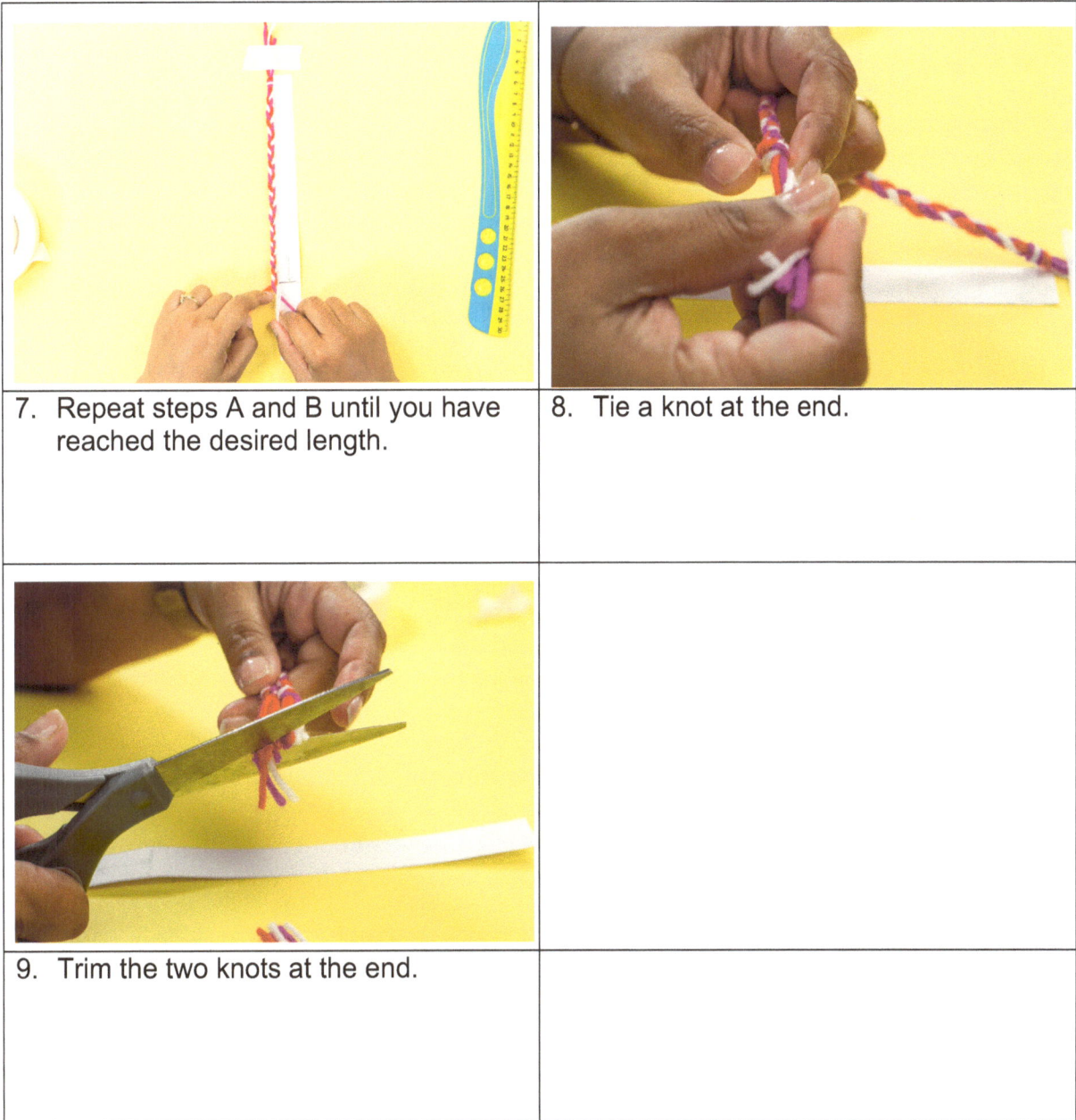

7. Repeat steps A and B until you have reached the desired length.

8. Tie a knot at the end.

9. Trim the two knots at the end.

49. Turtle

Art and Craft for Elementary School

MATERIALS:

Craft Box
- Three craft sticks
- Three colours of yarn (your choice of colour)

Recyclables and Other Materials and Tools
- Black marker or pen
- Scissors

1. Make an 'X' with two sticks and glue them together. Draw the turtle's "toes" at the end of the sticks.

2. Glue the third stick under the "X" as seen above.
3. Draw eyes and a smile at one end and a tail on the other end of the third stick.

4. Tie a piece of yarn around one stick and wrap it around the entire turtle. The wrapping pattern is "Over two and under one" Go around a few times until you return to where you started.

5. Tie the end of the yarn to the previous knot and trim. Repeat steps three and four with the other length of yarn until you have covered the turtle's "body".

Playing with Fabric

Many types of fabric can be used in our projects. You can also recycle used fabric such as denim, t-shirts and old shirts.

50. Decorate your art bag

MATERIALS

Recyclables and Other Materials and Tools
- Art bag.
- Permanent markers
- One sheet copy paper
- One Piece of cardboard

1. Use your marker to practice making doodles, or patterns on the paper

2. Once you are happy with your design, place the cardboard inside the bag. Write your name and draw your design on your bag.

Art and Craft for Elementary School

51. Tic Tac Toe Game 2

MATERIALS

Craft Box
- One piece felt square 4" x 4" (10cm x 10cm).

Recyclables and Other Materials and Tools
- Ten bottle caps
- Permanent marker
- Ruler

1. Use the marker and your ruler to make a grid on the felt, as shown above.

2. Draw "O"s and "X"s on the bottle caps. (five each)

   Easy peasy lemon squeezy – DONE!

Playing with Fabric

52. Patterned Tea Towel

Materials:

Recyclables and Other Materials and Tools
- Tea towel or
- Cotton fabric 12" x 18" (use 30 cm x 46cm)
- Paint (Acrylic)
- Paint Brush
- Paper roll or other pattern

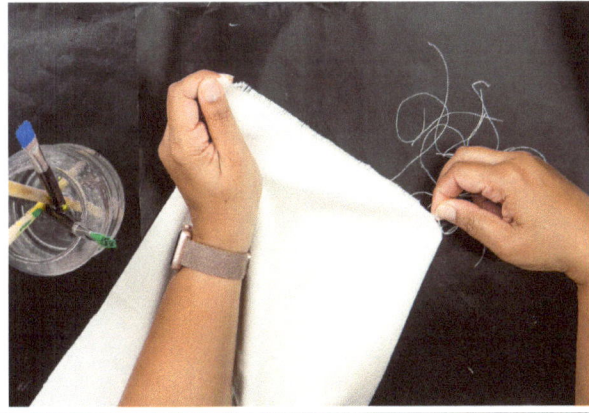

1. If you are using unsewn fabric, pull the strings at the end to form a fringe

2. Bend the middle of the roll to create a heart shape as shown.

3. Apply paint to the outer rim of the roll.

4. Stamp the paint unto the fabric or tea towel. Continue stamping using three colours until you are happy with the result.

73

Templates

Fan
Pinwheel
Basket

6 inches by 6 inches
or 15 cm by 15cm

Templates

Butterfly Puppet
Butterfly Mobile

Bee Puppet

Folded Butterfly

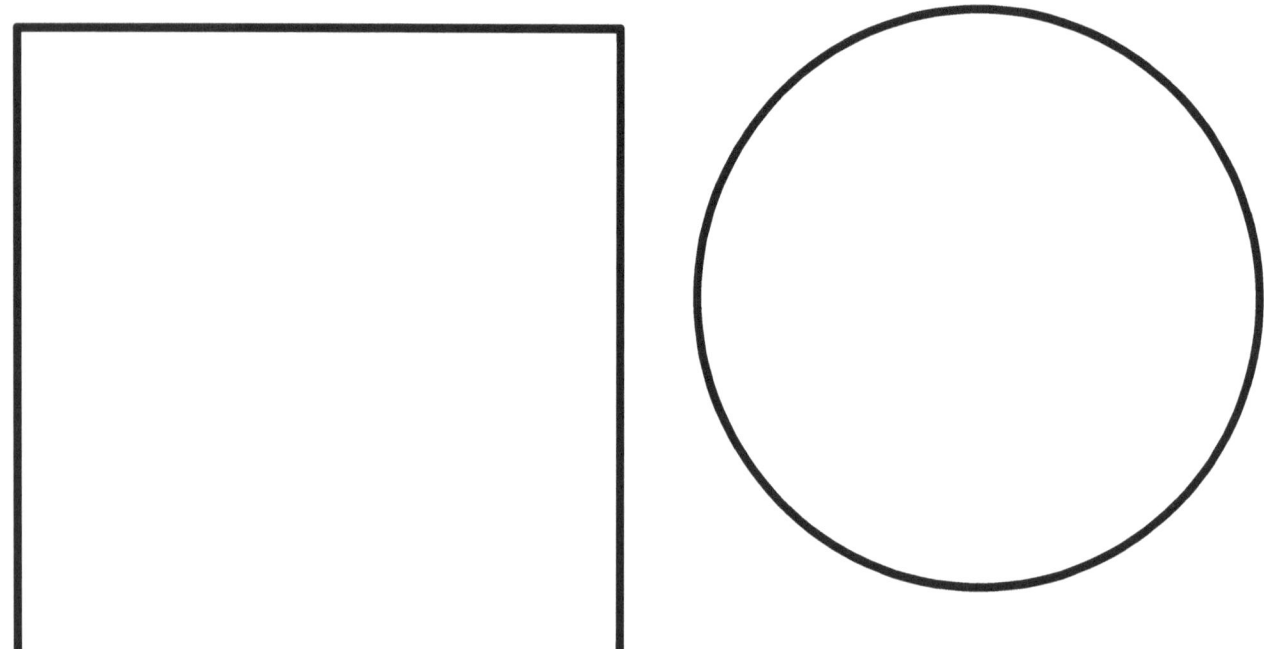

Templates

Jellyfish Sun-catcher

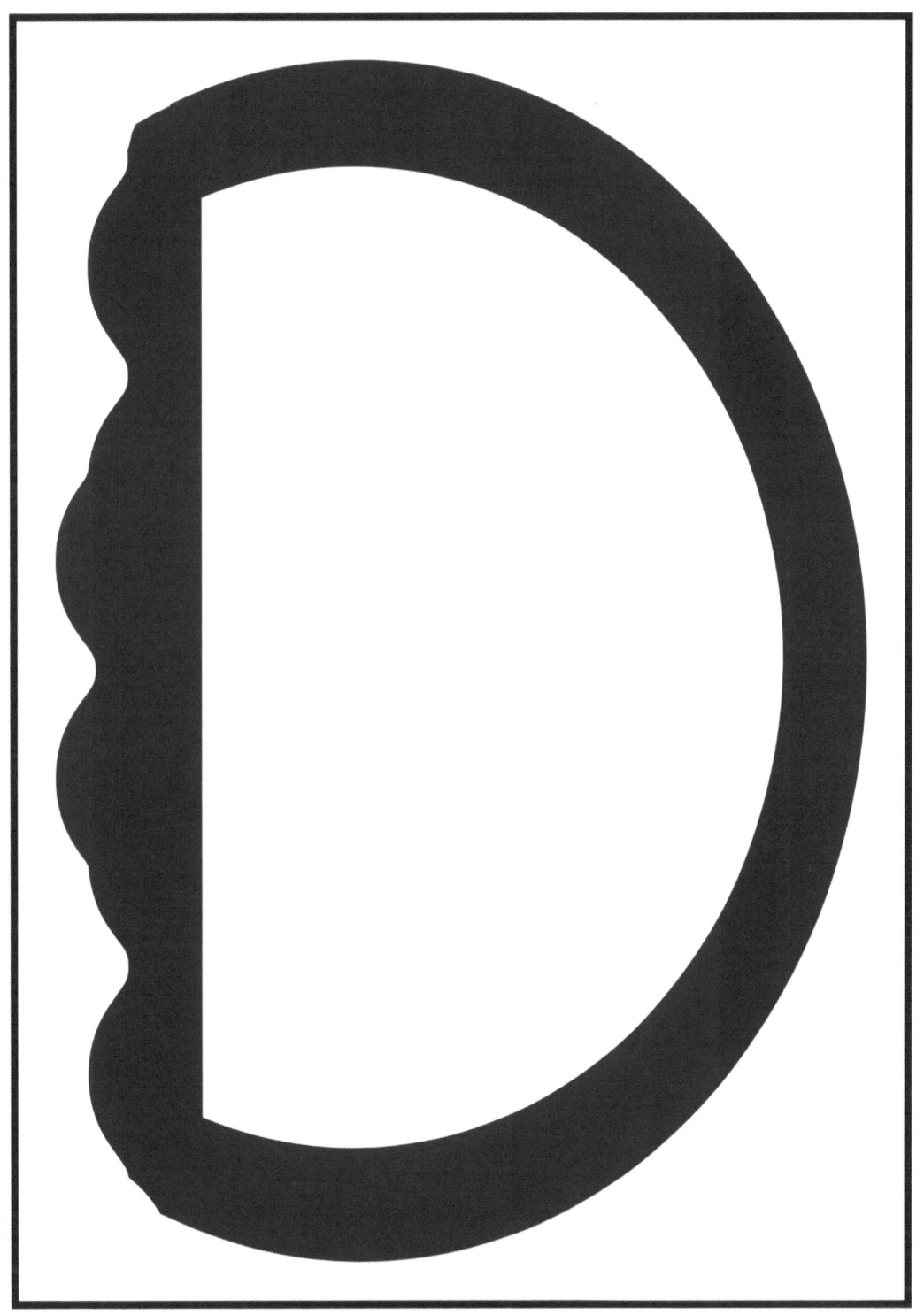

Door Hanger

Art and Craft for Elementary School

Ninja Star

Templates

Heart Card

Candle Card

Art and Craft for Elementary School

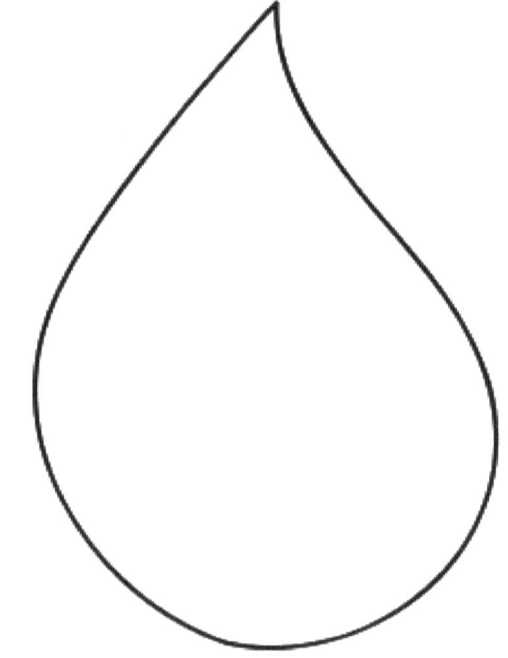

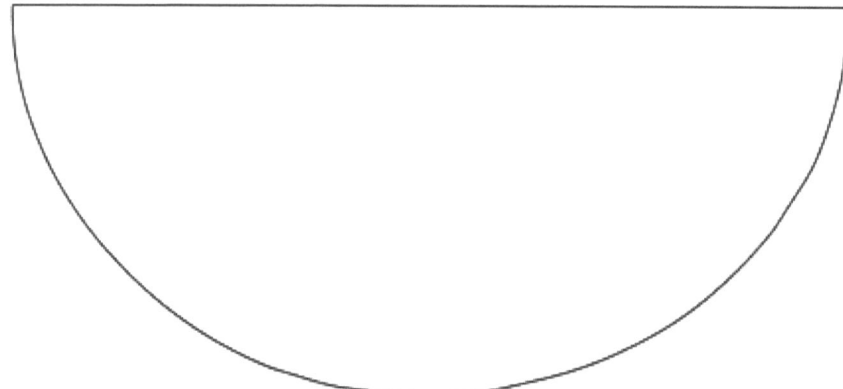

www.ingramcontent.com/pod-product-compliance
Lightning Source LLC
Chambersburg PA
CBHW050748110526
44591CB00002B/11